Grandma's
Best Recipes

Grandma's
Best Recipes

Traditional comfort food
just like Grandma used to make

This edition published in 2010
LOVE FOOD is an imprint of Parragon Books Ltd

Parragon
Queen Street House
4 Queen Street
Bath BA1 1HE, UK

ISBN: 978-1-4454-1159-0

Printed in China

Internal design by Jane Bozzard-Hill
Photography by Clive Bozzard-Hill
Home economists: Sandra Baddeley and Valerie Barrett
Introduction by Pamela Gwyther

Notes for the Reader

This book uses both metric and imperial measurements. Follow the same units of measurement throughout; do not mix metric and imperial. All spoon measurements are level: teaspoons are assumed to be 5 ml, and tablespoons are assumed to be 15 ml. Unless otherwise stated, milk is assumed to be full fat, eggs and individual vegetables are medium, and pepper is freshly ground black pepper.

The times given are an approximate guide only. Preparation times differ according to the techniques used by different people and the cooking times may also vary from those given. Optional ingredients, variations or serving suggestions have not been included in the calculations.

Recipes using raw or very lightly cooked eggs should be avoided by infants, the elderly, pregnant women, convalescents and anyone suffering from an illness. Pregnant and breastfeeding women are advised to avoid eating peanuts and peanut products. Sufferers from nut allergies should be aware that some of the ready-made ingredients used in the recipes in this book may contain nuts. Always check the packaging before use.

$\mathcal{C}$ONTENTS

6   Introduction

10   *Chapter One:* Grandma's Comfort Food

56   *Chapter Two:* Grandma's Travels

96   *Chapter Three:* Grandma's Festive Fare

142   *Chapter Four:* Grandma's Just Desserts

178   *Chapter Five:* Grandma's Baking Day

222   Index

INTRODUCTION

This is a book about all of our favourite childhood food memories, and it will give you the opportunity to create dishes 'just like Grandma used to make'. It will conjure up all the wonderful food smells that would always be present when we went to visit our grandparents as children, and the warm home-cooked meals that were waiting for us. It would be particularly welcoming to arrive when Grandma had just been baking and there was a selection of cakes and biscuits, and even freshly baked bread to smother with butter and eat fresh from the oven. Grandma's food was always a comfort; just the right thing to cheer you up, soothe a cold or even help heal a broken heart. Like Grandma herself, her food was always there and could be relied upon in all circumstances.

'Grandma's food was always a comfort – just the thing to cheer you up'

For many of us, our childhoods were very much linked to our grandparents. When we visited them for Christmas and other holidays, all the traditional foods would appear as if by magic. It is only with hindsight that we appreciate the amount of planning and hard work that went into making our perfect holidays. Often we would not only be able to eat the food but also have the thrill of helping to make it. Somehow, Grandma always had time to allow us to roll out the pastry and biscuits and help mix the cakes. She even allowed us to lick the wooden spoon and scrape the mixing bowl to try the delicious mix before it went in the oven. It was here that many of us learned to cook as Grandma was able to spend time with us and pass on the considerable knowledge that she had acquired over the years.

Weekends spent at our grandparents' often meant a traditional roast would be served. In addition to a huge joint of meat, there would be all the accompaniments: the vegetables, roast potatoes and parsnips, oodles of gravy and always Yorkshire pudding, even when it wasn't beef. The meal would always be followed by a wonderful pudding – apple pie, a crumble or maybe a lemon meringue pie. When there was a celebration, like a birthday, there might even be a Black Forest gateau or an iced cake with candles for the birthday girl or boy to blow out.

The food Grandma prepared for everyday meals was simpler. Firstly, because times were harder in her day, the maximum use was made of leftovers, such as shepherd's pie, using the remnants from the Sunday roast. Meals tended to be rather heavy as people often had to do more physical work and didn't have cars, so would walk relatively long distances. Casseroles and stews using the cheaper cuts of meat were prepared and cooked for a long time in a slow oven so that the meat would be really tender. Sausages and potatoes were also popular as they were filling and economical. Vegetables were often home-grown so they were fresh and in season. Some of the surplus vegetable and fruits would be preserved for use later in the year – fruit was turned into jam and vegetables were salted or made into chutneys.

Today's generation of grandmothers is more likely to be engaged full-time in the workplace and trying to juggle home, family, work, hobbies, interests and travels abroad. Her time for cooking has been reduced and she probably saves the traditional foods for special occasions and chooses quicker and healthier recipes in her day-to-day cooking. Her food habits are changing too, influenced by travel to far-away places and sampling the local fare. Today's multicultural society also means

*'Like Grandma herself, her food could be relied upon
in all circumstances'*

that we eat different foods on different occasions and celebrate new festivals. We also have a wider variety of food ingredients available, making many exciting new recipes and exotic meals far more accessible.

As the years have passed, our eating habits have changed. Foods that would have been considered exotic twenty years ago have become part of our everyday life – and comfort foods in their own right. Chicken tikka masala has overtaken roast beef as our nation's favourite dish. Pizza is another example of a food which has been absorbed into our national food identity along with others, such as chicken Kiev, spaghetti Bolognese and chilli con carne. This is a result of the changing population of our own country and the fact that many of us now have the opportunity to travel throughout the world. Most of our grandparents did not get the chance to journey much further than their own backyards, but global travel has widened the range of food experiences for today's generation. South American, Asian and Eastern European foods have all become part of our regular diet in recent years.

The way we eat has also changed through recent years. Although many will say that it is a shame that families tend not to sit down together for meals anymore, some food habits have changed for the better. We eat a lighter diet and consume more good-quality fresh fruits and vegetables now that these are available throughout the year. We are much more aware of what foods are good for us, although our busy lifestyles often lead us to make unwise food choices and to give in to the convenience of ready-made food or takeaways.

Obviously at the weekends, when we have more time, the favourite recipes come into their own. Although they may have a newer twist or include a prepared ingredient, like ready-to-use pastry, they are essentially the foods we ate in our childhood. Also, when there is a birthday or anniversary we tend to make more of an effort in preparing the food and are more extravagant with its selection. This is also the time when we might bake, providing family or friends with something delicious, like gingerbread or coffee and walnut cake, to accompany a cup of tea or coffee. Some people spend some of their time at weekends preparing home-cooked food and then freezing it for later in the week. In order to do this you need to be organised and have large saucepans so that you can make dishes in large quantities, but it is worth the effort.

Comfort foods are the old favourites: the meals that are particularly familiar to us, give us a warm feeling and soothe our souls. Grandma made these for us when we were young, so the good feelings associated with them are still there. When we are upset, worried or depressed, simple food like a warming chicken soup is just what is needed. Dishes that you can eat with your hands, such as bacon butties or welsh rarebit, are just the thing when you don't feel like sitting at the table with a knife and fork. A stew is

GRANDMA'S COMFORT FOOD

an excellent standby for a cold winter's day and provides a great opportunity to get the family sitting around the table, eating and discussing the day's occurrences. Other familiar foods, like traditional roast chicken, fish pie and baked potatoes, are all covered in this chapter so, whenever you need them, you'll have heartening recipes to hand, just like the ones your Grandma might have cooked for you.

LEEK & POTATO SOUP

SERVES 4–6
55 g/2 oz butter
I onion, chopped
3 leeks, sliced
225 g/8 oz potatoes, cut into
   2-cm/¾-inch cubes

850 ml/1½ pints vegetable stock
salt and pepper
150 ml/5 fl oz single cream (optional)
fresh flat-leaf parsley sprigs, to garnish
crusty bread, to serve

GRANDMA'S TIPS
This soup needs some seasoning to bring the flavours together. However, if you want to cut down on your salt intake, add a splash of lemon juice instead as an alternative to enhance those lovely flavours.

1 Melt the butter in a large saucepan over a medium heat, add the onion, leeks and potatoes and sauté gently for 2–3 minutes, until soft but not brown. Pour in the stock, bring to the boil, then reduce the heat and simmer, covered, for 15 minutes.

2 Remove from the heat and liquidize the soup in the saucepan using a hand-held stick blender if you have one. Alternatively, pour into a blender, liquidize until smooth and return to the rinsed-out saucepan.

3 Heat the soup, season to taste with salt and pepper and serve in warmed bowls. Swirl with the cream, if using, garnish with parsley and serve with crusty bread.

CREAM OF CHICKEN
SOUP

SERVES 4
3 tbsp butter
4 shallots, chopped
1 leek, trimmed and sliced
450 g/1 lb skinless chicken breasts,
   chopped
600 ml/1 pint chicken stock

1 tbsp chopped fresh parsley
1 tbsp chopped fresh thyme
salt and pepper
175 ml/6 fl oz double cream
sprigs of fresh thyme, to garnish
fresh crusty rolls, to serve

GRANDMA'S TIPS

If you have just cooked a whole chicken for a meal, you can make a stock with the leftovers. Place the carcass in a large saucepan of water along with a chopped onion, carrot and celery stick. Bring to the boil, then simmer for 1–1¼ hours. Strain and carefully remove any meat from the bones and set aside. Make the soup according to the recipe, adding the cooked chicken pieces either before blending or just before serving.

1 Melt the butter in a large saucepan over a medium heat. Add the shallots and cook, stirring, for 3 minutes, until slightly softened. Add the leek and cook for a further 5 minutes, stirring. Add the chicken, stock and herbs, and season with salt and pepper. Bring to the boil, then lower the heat and simmer for 25 minutes, until the chicken is tender and cooked through. Remove from the heat and leave to cool for 10 minutes.

2 Transfer the soup into a food processor and blend until smooth (you may need to do this in batches). Return the soup to the pan and warm over a low heat for 5 minutes.

3 Stir in the cream and cook for a further 2 minutes, then remove from the heat and ladle into serving bowls. Garnish with sprigs of thyme and serve with fresh crusty rolls.

WELSH RAREBIT

SERVES 4
4 slices thick white or brown bread
225 g/8 oz mature Cheddar cheese,
  grated
25 g/1 oz butter

3 tbsp beer
salt and pepper
½ tsp dry mustard powder
1 egg, beaten

1 Toast the bread under a medium grill on 1 side only.

2 Put the cheese into a saucepan and add the butter and beer. Heat slowly over a low heat, stirring continuously. Add some salt and pepper and the mustard powder and stir well until the mixture is thick and creamy. Remove from the heat and allow to cool slightly before mixing in the egg.

3 Spread the rarebit over the untoasted side of the bread and place under the hot grill until golden and bubbling. Serve at once.

BACON BUTTIES

SERVES 1
2 smoked bacon rashers
15 g/½ oz butter, softened
2 slices thick white or brown bread

pepper
1 tomato, sliced (optional)
sauce of choice (brown sauce, tomato
    ketchup or mustard)

GRANDMA'S TIPS

These traditional 'door-step' butties can be made using thinly sliced bread with the addition of lettuce to make a BLT (bacon, lettuce and tomato) – the sauce is optional. For an even more exotic sarnie, add some slices of avocado.

1 Cut the rashers of bacon in half so that you have 2 pieces of back bacon and 2 pieces of streaky.

2 Place the bacon under a hot grill and grill, turning frequently, until the bacon is cooked and as crispy as you like it.

3 Meanwhile, butter the bread.

4 Place 2 pieces of bacon on one slice of bread and season with a grinding of pepper. Add the tomato, if using, and the sauce. Top with the remaining bacon and the other slice of bread and eat immediately.

ROAST CHICKEN

SERVES 6
1 free-range chicken, weighing 2.25 kg/
  5 lb
55 g/2 oz butter
2 tbsp chopped fresh lemon thyme

salt and pepper
1 lemon, quartered
125 ml/4 fl oz white wine
6 fresh thyme sprigs, to garnish

GRANDMA'S TIPS

This is the quintessential roast chicken recipe. If you want even more flavour to the bird, stuff it with a finely chopped onion, the grated rind and juice of 1 lemon and some fresh thyme leaves mixed with a few soft breadcrumbs. For an even more robust variation, stuff the bird with 40 cloves of garlic – it will be delicious and milder than you might think, as the cooking renders the garlic sweet and not so pungent.

1 Preheat the oven to 220°C/425°F/Gas Mark 7. Make sure the chicken is clean, wiping it inside and out using kitchen paper, and place in a roasting tin.

2 Place the butter in a bowl and soften with a fork, then mix in the thyme and season well with salt and pepper. Butter the chicken all over with the herb butter, inside and out, and place the lemon quarters inside the body cavity. Pour the wine over the chicken.

3 Roast the chicken in the centre of the oven for 20 minutes. Reduce the temperature to 190°C/375°F/Gas Mark 5 and continue to roast for a further 1¼ hours, basting frequently. Cover with foil if the skin begins to brown too much. If the tin dries out, add a little more wine or water.

4 Test that the chicken is cooked by piercing the thickest part of the leg with a sharp knife or skewer and making sure the juices run clear. Remove from the oven.

5 Remove the chicken from the roasting tin and place on a warmed serving plate to rest, covered with foil, for 10 minutes before carving.

6 Place the roasting tin on the top of the hob and bubble the pan juices gently over a low heat until they have reduced and are thick and glossy. Season to taste with salt and pepper.

7 Serve the chicken with the pan juices and scatter with the thyme sprigs.

CHICKEN, MUSHROOM & TARRAGON PIE

SERVES 4–6

filling
1 chicken, about 1.5 kg/3 lb 5 oz
2 fresh tarragon sprigs
1 Spanish onion, cut into wedges
300 ml/10 fl oz water
salt and pepper
25 g/1 oz butter
175 g/6 oz chestnut mushrooms, sliced
2 tbsp plain flour
55 g/2 oz frozen or shelled fresh peas
1 tbsp chopped fresh tarragon

pastry
225 g/8 oz plain flour,
    plus extra for dusting
pinch of salt
175 g/6 oz butter
4 tbsp iced water
1 egg, lightly beaten

1 Preheat the oven to 200°C/400°F/Gas Mark 6. Put the chicken, tarragon sprigs and onion into a casserole, add the water and season. Cover and bake for 1½ hours. Remove the chicken. Strain the juices into a measuring jug and chill.

2 To make the pastry, sift the flour with the salt into a bowl and add the butter and water. Mix to a firm but slightly lumpy dough, adding more iced water if necessary. Roll out into a rectangle on a lightly floured surface, then fold the top third down and the bottom third up. Give the dough a quarter turn, roll out and fold again. Repeat once more, then wrap and chill for 30 minutes.

3 Discard the chicken skin, cut off the meat and dice. Skim off the fat from the cooking juices and make up to 300 ml/10 fl oz with water.

4 Melt the butter in a pan. Cook the mushrooms over a medium heat for 3 minutes. Stir in the flour for 1 minute, then gradually stir in the cooking juices. Bring to the boil, add the chicken, peas and tarragon and season to taste. Transfer to a large pie dish and cool.

5 Preheat the oven to 200°C/400°F/Gas Mark 6. Roll out the pastry to 2.5 cm/1 inch larger than the top of the dish. Cut out a 15-mm/⅝-inch strip all the way around. Brush the rim of the dish with water and press the strip on to it. Brush with water and lift the remaining dough on top. Trim off the excess and crimp the edges to seal. Make a slit in the centre and brush with beaten egg. Roll out the trimmings and use to decorate the pie, then brush with beaten egg. Bake for 40 minutes, until golden. Serve immediately.

ROAST BEEF

SERVES 8

1 prime rib of beef joint, weighing
  2.7 kg/6 lb
salt and pepper
2 tsp dry English mustard

3 tbsp plain flour
300 ml/10 fl oz red wine
300 ml/10 fl oz beef stock
2 tsp Worcestershire sauce (optional)
Yorkshire pudding, to serve

GRANDMA'S TIPS

Instead of making a traditional gravy, you can just pour off the fat and add enough red wine to deglaze the pan. Season to taste and serve immediately. This is known as a 'jus'.

1 Preheat the oven to 230°C/450°F/Gas Mark 8.

2 Season the meat to taste with salt and pepper. Rub in the mustard and 1 tablespoon of the flour.

3 Place the meat in a roasting tin large enough to hold it comfortably and roast in the oven for 15 minutes. Reduce the temperature to 190°C/375°F/Gas Mark 5 and cook for 15 minutes per 450 g/1 lb, plus 15 minutes (1¾ hours for this joint) for rare beef or 20 minutes per 450 g/1 lb, plus 20 minutes (2 hours 20 minutes) for medium beef. Baste the meat from time to time to keep it moist, and if the tin becomes too dry, add a little stock or red wine.

4 Remove the meat from the oven and place on a warmed serving plate, cover with foil and leave in a warm place for 10–15 minutes.

5 To make the gravy, pour off most of the fat from the tin, leaving behind the meat juices and the sediment. Place the tin on the hob over a medium heat and scrape all the sediment from the base of the tin. Sprinkle in the remaining flour and quickly mix it into the juices with a small whisk. When you have a smooth paste, gradually add the wine and most of the stock, whisking constantly. Bring to the boil, then reduce the heat to a gentle simmer and cook for 2–3 minutes. Season to taste with salt and pepper and add the remaining stock, if needed, and a little Worcestershire sauce, if you like.

6 When ready to serve, carve the meat into slices and serve on warmed plates. Pour the gravy into a warmed jug and take direct to the table. Serve with Yorkshire pudding.

BEEF STEW WITH
HERB DUMPLINGS

SERVES 6
3 tbsp olive oil
2 onions, finely sliced
2 garlic cloves, chopped
1 kg/2 lb 4 oz good-quality braising steak
2 tbsp plain flour
salt and pepper
300 ml/10 fl oz beef stock
bouquet garni
150 ml/5 fl oz red wine
1 tbsp chopped fresh parsley, to garnish

for the herb dumplings
115 g/4 oz self-raising flour, plus extra
  for shaping
55 g/2 oz suet or vegetable shortening
1 tsp mustard
1 tbsp chopped fresh parsley
1 tsp chopped fresh sage
salt and pepper
4 tbsp cold water

GRANDMA'S TIPS

You can make the stew the day before and refrigerate it overnight. Reheat 20 minutes before you're ready to add the dumplings, and proceed with the recipe. This will enhance the flavour of the stew and makes for fresh and light dumplings. You can vary the herbs used – try rosemary or thyme – and add some crushed garlic if you like.

1 Preheat the oven to 150°C/300°F/Gas Mark 2.

2 Heat 1 tablespoon of the oil in a large frying pan and fry the onion and garlic until soft and brown. Remove from the pan using a slotted spoon and place in a large casserole dish.

3 Trim the meat and cut into thick strips. Using the remaining oil, fry the meat in the frying pan over a high heat, stirring well until it is brown all over.

4 Sprinkle in the flour and stir well to prevent lumps. Season well with salt and pepper.

5 Over a medium heat, pour in the stock, stirring all the time to make a smooth sauce, then continue to heat until boiling.

6 Carefully turn the contents of the frying pan into the casserole dish. Add the bouquet garni and the wine. Cover and cook gently for 2–2½ hours.

7 Start making the dumplings 20 minutes before the stew is ready. Place the flour, suet, mustard, parsley, sage, and salt and pepper to taste in a bowl and mix well. Just before adding the dumplings to the stew, add enough of the water to the mixture to form a firm but soft dough. Break the dough into 12 pieces and roll them into round dumplings (you might need some flour on your hands for this).

8 Remove the stew from the oven, check the seasoning, discard the bouquet garni and add the dumplings, pushing them down under the liquid. Cover and return the dish to the oven, continuing to cook for 15 minutes until the dumplings have doubled in size.

9 Serve piping hot with the parsley scattered over the top.

STEAK & KIDNEY PIE

SERVES 4–6

butter, for greasing
700 g/1 lb 9 oz braising steak, trimmed
    and cut into 4-cm/1½-inch pieces
3 lambs' kidneys, cored and cut into
    2.5-cm/1-inch pieces
2 tbsp plain flour, plus extra for dusting
salt and pepper

3 tbsp vegetable oil
1 onion, roughly chopped
1 garlic clove, finely chopped
125 ml/4 fl oz red wine
450 ml/16 fl oz stock
1 bay leaf
400 g/14 oz ready-made puff pastry
1 egg, beaten

1 Preheat the oven to 160°C/325°F/Gas Mark 3. Grease a 1.2-litre/2-pint pie dish.

2 Put the prepared meat with the flour and salt and pepper in a large plastic bag and shake until all the meat is well coated.

3 Heat the oil in a flameproof casserole over a high heat and brown the meat in batches. Remove from the casserole with a slotted spoon and keep warm. Fry the onion and garlic in the casserole for 2–3 minutes until softening.

4 Stir in the wine and scrape the base of the pan to release the sediment. Pour in the stock, stirring constantly, and bring to the boil. Bubble for 2–3 minutes. Add the bay leaf and return the meat to the casserole. Cover and cook in the centre of the oven for 1½–2 hours. Check the seasoning, then remove the bay leaf. Leave the meat to cool, preferably overnight, to develop the flavours.

5 Preheat the oven to 200°C/400°F/Gas Mark 6.

6 Roll out the pastry on a lightly floured work surface to about 7 cm/2¾ inches larger than the pie dish. Cut off a 3-cm/1¼-inch strip from the edge. Moisten the rim of the dish and press the pastry strip onto it. Place the pie funnel in the centre of the dish and spoon in the steak and kidney filling. Don't overfill, keeping any extra gravy to serve separately. Moisten the pastry collar with water and put on the pastry lid, taking care to fit it carefully around the pie funnel. Crimp the edges of the pastry firmly and glaze with the egg.

7 Place the pie on a tray towards the top of the oven for about 30 minutes. The pie should be golden brown and the filling bubbling hot; cover it with foil and reduce the temperature if the pastry is getting too brown.

SHEPHERD'S PIE

SERVES 6
1 tbsp olive oil
2 onions, finely chopped
2 garlic cloves, finely chopped
675 g/1 lb 8 oz good-quality lamb mince
2 carrots, finely chopped
salt and pepper
1 tbsp plain flour
225 ml/8 fl oz beef or chicken stock
125 ml/4 fl oz red wine
Worcestershire sauce (optional)

mashed potato
675g g/1 lb 8 oz floury potatoes, such as
    King Edward, Maris Piper or Desirée,
    peeled and cut into even-sized chunks
55 g/2 oz butter
2 tbsp cream or milk
salt and pepper

GRANDMA'S TIPS

*To make a cottage pie, use
minced beef instead of the lamb.
Instead of the basic mashed
potato topping, you could try
using a mixture of mashed
potatoes and carrot or parsnip.
Alternatively, substitute grated
potato for the mashed potatoes
for a 'rösti-style' topping.*

1 Preheat the oven to 180°C/350°F/Gas Mark 4.

2 Heat the oil in a large, flameproof casserole dish and fry the onion until softened, then add the garlic and stir well.

3 Raise the heat and add the meat. Cook quickly to brown the meat all over, stirring continually. Add the carrots and season well with salt and pepper.

4 Stir in the flour and add the stock and wine. Stir well and heat until simmering and thickened.

5 Cover the casserole dish and cook in the oven for about 1 hour. Check the consistency from time to time and add a little more stock or wine if required. The meat mixture should be quite thick but not dry. Season with salt and pepper to taste and add a little Worcestershire sauce, if desired.

6 While the meat is cooking, make the mashed potato. Cook the potatoes in a large saucepan of boiling salted water for 15–20 minutes. Drain well and mash with a potato masher until smooth. Add the butter and cream and season well with salt and pepper.

7 Spoon the lamb mixture into an ovenproof serving dish and spread or pipe the potato on top.

8 Increase the oven temperature to 200°C/400°F/Gas Mark 6 and cook the pie for 15–20 minutes at the top of the oven until golden brown. You might like to finish it off under a medium grill for a really crisp brown topping to the potato.

LAMB SHANKS WITH CANNELLINI BEANS

SERVES 4

250 g/9 oz cannellini beans,
    soaked overnight
2 tbsp sunflower oil
1 large onion, thinly sliced
4 carrots, chopped
2 celery sticks, thinly sliced
1 garlic clove, chopped

4 large lamb shanks
400 g/14 oz canned chopped tomatoes
300 ml/10 fl oz red wine
finely pared zest and juice of 1 orange
2 bay leaves
3 rosemary sprigs
225 ml/8 fl oz water
salt and pepper

GRANDMA'S TIPS

If you find the red wine sauce too rich, try replacing this with some stock. Also, if you are a fan of vegetables, try adding more varieties into the stew with the carrots and celery.

1 Preheat the oven to 160°C/325°F/Gas Mark 3. Drain the soaked beans and rinse under cold running water. Put in a large pan of cold water, bring to the boil and skim off any scum, then boil rapidly for 10 minutes. Drain and set aside.

2 Meanwhile, heat the oil in a large, flameproof casserole, add the onion, and cook for 5 minutes, or until softened. Add the carrots and celery and cook for a further 5 minutes, or until beginning to soften and the onion is beginning to brown. Add the garlic and cook for a further 1 minute. Push the vegetables to the sides of the pan.

3 Add the lamb shanks to the pan and cook for about 5 minutes, until browned on all sides. Add the beans to the pan with the tomatoes, wine and orange zest and juice, and stir together. Add the bay leaves and rosemary. Pour in the water so that the liquid comes halfway up the shanks. Season with pepper but do not add salt as this will stop the beans from softening.

4 Bring to the boil, then cover the pan and cook in the oven for about 1 hour. Turn the shanks over in the stock then continue cooking for 1½ hours until the lamb and beans are tender. Remove the bay leaves, then taste and add salt and pepper if necessary. Serve hot.

SAUSAGE & BEAN CASSEROLE

SERVES 4

8 Italian sausages
3 tbsp olive oil
I large onion, chopped
2 garlic cloves, chopped
I green pepper, deseeded and sliced
225g/8 oz fresh tomatoes, skinned
   and chopped or 400 g/14 oz canned
   chopped tomatoes

2 tbsp sun-dried tomato paste
400 g/14 oz canned cannellini beans,
   drained
mashed potatoes, to serve

1 Prick the sausages all over with a fork. Heat 2 tablespoons of the oil in a large heavy-based frying pan. Add the sausages and cook over a low heat, turning frequently, for 10–15 minutes, until evenly browned and cooked through. Remove them from the frying pan and keep warm. Drain off the oil and wipe out the pan with kitchen paper.

2 Heat the remaining oil in the frying pan. Add the onion, garlic and green pepper to the frying pan and cook for 5 minutes, stirring occasionally, or until softened.

3 Add the tomatoes to the frying pan and leave the mixture to simmer for about 5 minutes, stirring occasionally, or until slightly reduced and thickened.

4 Stir the sun-dried tomato paste, cannellini beans and sausages into the mixture in the frying pan. Cook for 4–5 minutes, or until the mixture is piping hot. Add 4–5 tablespoons of water if the mixture becomes too dry during cooking.

5 Transfer to serving plates and serve with mashed potatoes.

TOAD IN THE HOLE

SERVES 4
oil, for greasing
115 g/4 oz plain flour
pinch of salt

I egg, beaten
300 ml/10 fl oz milk
450 g/1 lb good-quality pork sausages
I tbsp vegetable oil

GRANDMA'S TIPS

Try making toad in the hole with meat balls instead of sausages. Fried onion rings can also be added to the dish before adding the batter.

1 Grease a 20 x 25-cm/8 x 10-inch ovenproof dish or roasting tin.

2 Make the batter by sifting the flour and salt into a mixing bowl. Make a well in the centre and add the beaten egg and half the milk. Carefully stir the liquid into the flour until the mixture is smooth. Gradually beat in the remaining milk. Leave to stand for 30 minutes.

3 Preheat the oven to 220°C/425°F/Gas Mark 7.

4 Prick the sausages and place them in the dish. Sprinkle over the oil and cook the sausages in the oven for 10 minutes until they are beginning to colour and the fat has started to run and is sizzling.

5 Remove from the oven and quickly pour the batter over the sausages. Return to the oven and cook for 35–45 minutes until the batter is well risen and golden brown. Serve immediately.

FISH & CHIPS

SERVES 2
vegetable oil, for deep-frying
3 large potatoes, such as Cara or Desirée
2 thick cod or haddock fillets,
   175 g/6 oz each

salt and pepper
175 g/6 oz self-raising flour, plus extra
   for dusting
200 ml/7 fl oz cold lager
lemon wedges, to serve

1 Heat the oil in a temperature-controlled deep-fat fryer to 120°C/250°F, or in a heavy-based saucepan, checking the temperature with a thermometer, to blanch the chips. Preheat the oven to 150°C/300°F/Gas Mark 2.

2 Peel the potatoes and cut into even-sized chips. Fry for about 8–10 minutes, depending on size, until softened but not coloured. Remove from the oil, drain on kitchen paper and place in a warm dish in the warm oven. Increase the temperature of the oil to 180–190°C/350–375°F, or until a cube of bread browns in 30 seconds.

3 Meanwhile, season the fish with salt and pepper and dust it lightly with a little flour.

4 Make a thick batter by sieving the flour into a bowl with a little salt and whisking in most of the lager. Check the consistency before adding the remainder: it should be very thick, like double cream.

5 Dip one fillet into the batter and allow it to be thickly coated. Carefully place the fish in the hot oil, then repeat with the other fillet.

6 Cook for 8–10 minutes, depending on the thickness of the fish. Turn the fillets over halfway through the cooking time. Remove the fish from the fryer or saucepan, drain and keep warm.

7 Make sure the oil temperature is still at 180°C/350°F and return the chips to the fryer or saucepan. Cook for a further 2–3 minutes until golden brown and crispy. Drain and season with salt and pepper before serving with the battered fish and lemon wedges for squeezing over.

FISHERMAN'S PIE

SERVES 6
butter, for greasing
900 g/2 lb white fish fillets,
 such as plaice, skinned
salt and pepper
150 ml/5 fl oz dry white wine
1 tbsp chopped fresh parsley,
 tarragon or dill

175 g/6 oz small mushrooms, sliced
100 g/3½ oz butter
175 g/6 oz cooked peeled prawns
40 g/1½ oz plain flour
125 ml/4 fl oz double cream
900 g/2 lb floury potatoes, such as King
 Edward, Maris Piper or Desirée, peeled
 and cut into even-sized chunks

1 Preheat the oven to 180°C/350°F/Gas Mark 4. Butter a 1.7-litre/3-pint baking dish.

2 Fold the fish fillets in half and place in the dish. Season well with salt and pepper, pour over the wine and scatter over the herbs.

3 Cover with foil and bake for 15 minutes until the fish starts to flake. Strain off the liquid and reserve for the sauce. Increase the oven temperature to 220°C/425°F/ Gas Mark 7.

4 Sauté the mushrooms in a frying pan with 15 g/½ oz of the butter and spoon over the fish. Scatter over the prawns.

5 Heat 55 g/2 oz of the butter in a saucepan and stir in the flour. Cook for a few minutes without browning, remove from the heat, then add the reserved cooking liquid gradually, stirring well between each addition.

6 Return to the heat and gently bring to the boil, still stirring to ensure a smooth sauce. Add the cream and season to taste with salt and pepper. Pour over the fish in the dish and smooth over the surface.

7 Make the mashed potato by cooking the potatoes in boiling salted water for 15–20 minutes. Drain well and mash with a potato masher until smooth. Season to taste with salt and pepper and add the remaining butter, stirring until melted.

8 Pile or pipe the potato onto the fish and sauce and bake for 10–15 minutes until golden brown.

SALMON FISHCAKES

SERVES 4
700 g/1 lb 9 oz skinless salmon fillet,
   cut into cubes
300 ml/10 fl oz full-fat milk
1 bay leaf
100 g/3 ½ oz broccoli, steamed until
   tender
700 g/1 lb 9 oz potatoes, boiled and
   mashed

2 tbsp finely chopped fresh parsley
4 tbsp wholemeal plain flour
pepper
1 egg yolk
2 large eggs, beaten
150 g/5 ½ oz fresh wholemeal
   breadcrumbs
2 tbsp olive oil

GRANDMA'S TIPS

These absolutely delicious fishcakes can be made more economical by using canned salmon. The broccoli can be replaced with sautéed leeks or even some sweetcorn, which the kids will love. For a more sophisticated flavour, chopped dill can be used instead of the parsley and the fishcakes can be served with a dill sauce or mayonnaise.

1 Preheat the oven to 200°C/400°F/Gas Mark 6. Put the salmon in a saucepan with the milk and bay leaf and bring slowly up to a simmer. Simmer for 2 minutes, then remove the saucepan from the heat, lift out and discard the bay leaf and leave the fish in the milk to cool. When cooled, lift out the fish with a slotted spoon onto kitchen paper to drain.

2 Flake the fish into a large bowl. Put the broccoli in a food processor and pulse until smooth. Add to the fish with the mashed potatoes, parsley, 1 tablespoon of the flour, and pepper to taste. Add the egg yolk and mix well. If the mixture is a little dry, add some of the poaching milk; if too wet, add a little more flour.

3 Divide the mixture into 12 portions and shape each portion into a cake. Put the beaten eggs, remaining flour and the breadcrumbs on 3 separate plates. Roll each fishcake in the flour, then in the beaten egg, and then in the breadcrumbs to coat.

4 Heat the oil in a non-stick baking tray in the preheated oven for 5 minutes. Add the fishcakes and bake for 10 minutes, then carefully turn the fishcakes over and bake for a further 10 minutes. Serve hot.

WINTER VEGETABLE COBBLER

SERVES 4
1 tbsp olive oil
1 garlic clove, crushed
8 small onions, halved
2 celery sticks, sliced
225 g/8 oz swede, chopped
2 carrots, sliced
½ small head of cauliflower, broken into
  florets
225 g/8 oz button mushrooms, sliced
400 g/14 oz canned chopped tomatoes
55 g/2 oz red lentils, rinsed
2 tbsp cornflour
3–4 tbsp water

300 ml/10 fl oz vegetable stock
2 tsp Tabasco sauce
2 tsp chopped fresh oregano
fresh oregano sprigs, to garnish

for the topping
225 g/8 oz self-raising flour
pinch of salt
4 tbsp butter
115 g/4 oz grated mature Cheddar
  cheese
2 tsp chopped fresh oregano
1 egg, lightly beaten
150 ml/5 fl oz milk

GRANDMA'S TIPS

This rib-sticking dish is just the thing for those cold winter evenings. The vegetables can be varied according to taste and season. You might like to make a curry-flavoured cobbler by using curry paste instead of the Tabasco sauce. The topping can be made with wholemeal flour instead of white for a healthier version.

1 Preheat the oven to 180°C/350°F/Gas Mark 4. Heat the oil in a large frying pan and cook the garlic and onions over a low heat for 5 minutes. Add the celery, swede, carrots and cauliflower and cook for 2–3 minutes.

2 Add the mushrooms, tomatoes and lentils. Place the cornflour and water in a bowl and mix to make a smooth paste. Stir into the frying pan with the stock, Tabasco and oregano. Transfer to an ovenproof dish, cover and bake in the preheated oven for 20 minutes.

3 To make the topping, sift the flour and salt into a bowl. Add the butter and rub it in, then stir in most of the cheese and oregano. Beat the egg with the milk in a small bowl and add enough to the dry ingredients to make a soft dough. Knead, then roll out on a lightly floured work surface to 1 cm/½ inch thick. Cut into 5-cm/2-inch rounds.

4 Remove the dish from the oven and increase the temperature to 200°C/400°F/ Gas Mark 6. Arrange the dough rounds around the edge of the dish, brush with the remaining egg and milk mixture and sprinkle with the reserved cheese. Cook for a further 10–12 minutes. Garnish with oregano sprigs and serve.

ROASTED BUTTERNUT SQUASH RISOTTO

SERVES 4

600 g/1 lb 5 oz butternut squash or
   pumpkin, peeled and cut into
   bite-sized pieces
4 tbsp olive oil
1 tsp clear honey
25 g/1 oz fresh basil, plus extra sprigs
   to garnish

25 g/1 oz fresh oregano
1 tbsp margarine
2 onions, finely chopped
450 g/1 lb arborio or other risotto rice
175 ml/6 fl oz dry white wine
1.2 litres/2 pints vegetable stock
salt and pepper

1 Preheat the oven to 200°C/400°F/Gas Mark 6. Put the squash into a roasting tin. Mix 1 tablespoon of the oil with the honey and spoon over the squash. Turn the squash to coat it in the mixture. Roast in the preheated oven for 30–35 minutes, or until tender.

2 Meanwhile, put the basil and oregano into a food processor with 2 tablespoons of the remaining oil and process until finely chopped and blended. Set aside.

3 Heat the margarine and remaining oil in a large, heavy-based saucepan over a medium heat. Add the onions and fry, stirring occasionally, for 8 minutes, or until soft and golden. Add the rice and cook for 2 minutes, stirring to coat the grains in the oil mixture.

4 Pour in the wine and bring to the boil. Reduce the heat slightly and cook until the wine is almost absorbed. Add the stock, a little at a time, and cook over a medium-low heat, stirring constantly, for 20 minutes.

5 Gently stir in the herb oil and squash until thoroughly mixed into the rice and cook for a further 5 minutes, or until the rice is creamy and cooked but retaining a little bite in the centre of the grain. Season well with salt and pepper before serving, garnished with sprigs of basil.

MACARONI CHEESE

SERVES 4
600 ml/1 pint milk
1 onion, peeled
8 peppercorns
1 bay leaf
55 g/2 oz butter
40 g/1½ oz plain flour
½ tsp ground nutmeg

5 tbsp double cream
pepper
100 g/3½ oz mature Cheddar cheese,
   grated
100 g/3½ oz Roquefort cheese, crumbled
350 g/12 oz dried macaroni
100 g/3½ oz Gruyère or Emmental
   cheese, grated

GRANDMA'S TIPS

Macaroni cheese is a great family favourite. This rich version using three varieties of cheese can be made simpler by using one cheese, such as Cheddar, and omitting the cream. You can also add some vegetables – steamed broccoli florets or baby spinach leaves will add colour and extra vitamins.

1 Put the milk, onion, peppercorns and bay leaf in a pan and bring to the boil. Remove from the heat and let stand for 15 minutes.

2 Melt the butter in a pan and stir in the flour until well combined and smooth. Cook over a medium heat, stirring constantly, for 1 minute. Remove from the heat. Strain the milk to remove the solids and stir a little into the butter and flour mixture until well incorporated. Return to the heat and gradually add the remaining milk, stirring constantly, until it has all been incorporated. Cook for a further 3 minutes, or until the sauce is smooth and thickened, then add the nutmeg, cream and pepper to taste. Add the Cheddar and Roquefort cheeses and stir until melted.

3 Meanwhile, bring a large pan of water to the boil. Add the macaroni, then return to the boil and cook for 8–10 minutes, or until just tender. Drain well and add to the cheese sauce. Stir well together.

4 Preheat the grill to high. Spoon the mixture into an ovenproof serving dish, then scatter over the Gruyère cheese and cook under the grill until bubbling and brown.

SOUFFLÉD BAKED
POTATOES

SERVES 4
2 baking potatoes, scrubbed
1 tbsp olive oil
2 tbsp full-fat milk
25 g/1 oz butter
25 g/1 oz Cheddar or Gruyère cheese, grated

1 large egg, separated
salt and pepper
2 slices ham, cooked turkey or unsmoked bacon, chopped
2 tbsp finely grated Parmesan cheese
salad, to serve

GRANDMA'S TIPS

Baked potatoes make for the perfect meal, particularly when they are stuffed with lots of tasty ingredients such as Bolognese or chilli sauce, flaked fish or ratatouille. Make sure the potatoes are baked through so that they're soft inside and the skins are firm and crispy, which makes them most delicious. You can even rub salt into the skins with the oil to enhance the flavour.

1 Preheat the oven to 200°C/400°F/Gas Mark 6. Prick the potatoes with a fork. Rub the oil all over the potatoes, place on a baking sheet and bake in the preheated oven for 1 hour, or until the flesh is soft.

2 Remove the potatoes from the oven, cut in half lengthways and carefully scoop out the flesh into a bowl, keeping the skins intact. Set the skins aside.

3 Add the milk, butter, Cheddar cheese and egg yolk to the potato and mash well. Season to taste with salt and pepper. Mix in the ham.

4 In a separate, grease-free bowl, whisk the egg white until stiff, then fold into the potato mixture.

5 Pile the potato mixture back into the skins and sprinkle over the Parmesan cheese. Return to the oven and bake for 20 minutes. Serve with salad.

PERFECT MASH

SERVES 4
900 g/2 lb floury potatoes, such as King
  Edward, Maris Piper or Desirée

4 tbsp butter
3 tbsp hot milk
salt and pepper

1 Peel the potatoes, placing them in cold water as you prepare the others to prevent them from going brown.

2 Cut the potatoes into even-sized chunks and cook in a large saucepan of boiling salted water over a medium heat, covered, for 20–25 minutes until they are tender. Test with the point of a knife, but make sure you test right in the middle to avoid lumps.

3 Remove the pan from the heat and drain the potatoes. Return the potatoes to the hot pan and mash with a potato masher until smooth.

4 Add the butter and continue to mash until it is all mixed in, then add the milk (it is better hot because the potatoes absorb it more quickly to produce a creamier mash).

5 Taste the mashed potatoes and season with salt and pepper as necessary. Serve at once.

CAULIFLOWER CHEESE

SERVES 4
1 cauliflower, trimmed and cut into florets
  (675 g/1 lb 8 oz prepared weight)
40 g/1½ oz butter
40 g/1½ oz plain flour

450 ml/16 fl oz milk
115 g/4 oz Cheddar cheese, finely grated
whole nutmeg, for grating
salt and pepper
1 tbsp grated Parmesan cheese

GRANDMA'S TIPS

Using a mixture of cauliflower and broccoli will give a more colourful dish. You can make it even more substantial by adding some fried sliced onions and fried bacon pieces before pouring over the sauce.

1 Cook the cauliflower in a saucepan of boiling salted water for 4–5 minutes. It should still be firm. Drain, place in a hot 1.4-litre/2½-pint gratin dish and keep warm.

2 Melt the butter in the rinsed-out saucepan over a medium heat and stir in the flour. Cook for 1 minute, stirring continuously.

3 Remove from the heat and stir in the milk gradually until you have a smooth consistency.

4 Return to a low heat and continue to stir while the sauce comes to the boil and thickens. Reduce the heat and simmer gently, stirring constantly, for about 3 minutes until the sauce is creamy and smooth.

5 Remove from the heat and stir in the Cheddar cheese and a good grating of the nutmeg. Taste and season well with salt and pepper.

6 Pour the hot sauce over the cauliflower, top with the Parmesan and place under a hot grill to brown. Serve immediately.

Grandmas in this day and age are jetting off or cruising all over the world. Travel is cheaper and easier than in the past, making it possible to visit far-off destinations with diverse cultures and foods. Countries like China, Mexico and the newly accessible Eastern European nations have all contributed to our varied cuisine. We have taken recipes from many different cultures and adapted them to our own way of eating. As our society becomes increasingly multicultural, ingredients for these types of recipes are becoming

GRANDMA'S TRAVELS

more readily available, not just from specialist shops but increasingly from main-stream supermarkets. Pasta has long been a favourite and spaghetti Bolognese is popular with adults and children alike. Pizza is an ideal finger food that can be made from scratch or using prepared pizza bases and topped with different ingredients so that everyone can choose their own. From further afield come chicken Kiev and beef goulash, together with beef enchiladas and chilli con carne, introducing newer flavours and spices into our diets. Pork chow mein and spicy beef with black bean sauce, with their use of eastern flavours and foodstuffs, are also included in this chapter.

SPAGHETTI
BOLOGNESE

SERVES 4
1 tbsp olive oil
1 onion, finely chopped
2 garlic cloves, chopped
1 carrot, chopped
1 celery stick, chopped
50 g/1¾ oz pancetta or streaky bacon, diced
350 g/12 oz lean fresh beef mince

400 g/14 oz canned chopped tomatoes
2 tsp dried oregano
125 ml/4 fl oz red wine
2 tbsp tomato purée
salt and pepper
350 g/12 oz dried spaghetti
freshly grated Parmesan cheese, to serve (optional)

GRANDMA'S TIPS

This is the world's favourite spaghetti dish, loved by adults and children alike. A good sauce takes time to make, but it's worth the effort. Prepare double quantities and freeze in individual portions so that you always have some on hand for a quick meal. Some recipes add chicken livers or mushrooms – the choice is up to you. Serve this dish piping hot with lots of grated cheese.

1 Heat the oil in a large frying pan over a low heat. Add the onion and cook for 3 minutes.

2 Add the garlic, carrot, celery and pancetta to the pan and sauté for 3–4 minutes, or until just starting to brown.

3 Add the beef and cook over a high heat for another 3 minutes, or until the meat has browned.

4 Stir in the tomatoes, oregano and red wine and bring to the boil. Reduce the heat and simmer for about 45 minutes.

5 Stir in the tomato purée and season with salt and pepper.

6 Bring a large pan of lightly salted water to the boil over a medium heat. Add the pasta and cook for about 8–10 minutes, or until tender, but still firm to the bite. Drain thoroughly.

7 Transfer the pasta to 4 serving plates and pour over the sauce. Toss to mix well and serve with Parmesan cheese, if you wish.

SPAGHETTI CARBONARA

SERVES 4
400 g/14 oz dried spaghetti
4 eggs
4 tbsp double cream
55 g/2 oz grated Parmesan cheese

55 g/2 oz grated pecorino cheese
salt and pepper
1 tbsp butter
150 g/5½ oz pancetta, finely diced

GRANDMA'S TIPS

This simple and delicious dish has room for extra ingredients. So try frying some small button mushrooms and adding them to the pasta and sauce to add flavour and texture.

1 Bring a large saucepan of lightly salted water to the boil. Add the spaghetti and cook according to the packet instructions or until tender, but firm to the bite. Meanwhile, stir together the eggs, cream, Parmesan cheese and pecorino cheese in a bowl. Add salt and pepper.

2 Melt the butter in a large saucepan, add the pancetta, and fry until crispy. Drain the spaghetti and add it to the pan while still dripping wet. Pour the cheese sauce over it. Remove the pan from the heat. Toss the spaghetti in the sauce until the eggs begin to thicken but are still creamy.

3 Serve on warmed plates, sprinkled with pepper.

VEGETABLE CANNELLONI

SERVES 4
12 dried cannelloni tubes
125 ml/4 fl oz olive oil,
    plus extra for brushing
1 aubergine
225 g/8 oz spinach
2 garlic cloves, crushed
1 tsp ground cumin
85 g/3 oz mushrooms, chopped
salt and pepper
55 g/2 oz mozzarella cheese, sliced
lamb's lettuce, to garnish

tomato sauce
1 tbsp olive oil
1 onion, chopped
2 garlic cloves, crushed
800 g/1 lb 12 oz canned chopped
    tomatoes
1 tsp caster sugar
2 tbsp chopped fresh basil

1 Preheat the oven to 190°C/375°F/Gas Mark 5. Bring a large heavy-bottom saucepan of lightly salted water to the boil. Add the cannelloni tubes, return to the boil and cook for 8–10 minutes, or until tender but still firm to the bite. Transfer the pasta to a plate and pat dry with kitchen paper. Brush a large ovenproof dish with oil.

2 Cut the aubergine into small dice. Heat the oil in a frying pan over a medium heat. Add the aubergine and cook, stirring frequently, for about 2–3 minutes.

3 Add the spinach, garlic, cumin and mushrooms and reduce the heat. Season to taste with salt and pepper and cook, stirring, for about 2–3 minutes. Spoon the mixture into the cannelloni tubes and put into the dish in a single layer.

4 To make the sauce, heat the oil in a pan over a medium heat. Add the onion and garlic and cook for 1 minute. Add the tomatoes, sugar and basil and bring to the boil. Reduce the heat and simmer for about 5 minutes. Spoon the sauce over the cannelloni tubes.

5 Arrange the mozzarella cheese on top of the sauce and bake in the preheated oven for about 30 minutes, or until the cheese is golden brown and bubbling. Serve garnished with lamb's lettuce.

LASAGNE AL FORNO

SERVES 4
2 tbsp olive oil
55 g/2 oz pancetta or rindless streaky
  bacon, chopped
1 onion, chopped
1 garlic clove, finely chopped
225 g/8 oz fresh beef mince
2 celery sticks, chopped
2 carrots, chopped
salt and pepper
pinch of sugar
½ tsp dried oregano
400 g/14 oz canned chopped tomatoes
225 g/8 oz dried no-precook lasagne
  sheets
115 g/4 oz freshly grated Parmesan
  cheese, plus extra for sprinkling

for the cheese sauce
300 ml/10 fl oz milk
1 bay leaf
6 black peppercorns
slice of onion
blade of mace
2 tbsp butter
3 tbsp plain flour
2 tsp Dijon mustard
70 g/2½ oz Cheddar cheese, grated
70 g/2½ oz Gruyère cheese, grated
salt and pepper

GRANDMA'S TIPS

This dish is quite complicated to make, as it requires you to make both a meat and a cheese sauce. To cheat a little, you can buy a ready-made cheese sauce to cut down on the preparation time. Make sure you use no-cook lasagne sheets as they will not need to be boiled before use.

1 Preheat the oven to 190°C/375°F/Gas Mark 5. Heat the olive oil in a large, heavy-based saucepan. Add the pancetta and cook over a medium heat, stirring occasionally, for 3 minutes, or until the fat begins to run. Add the onion and garlic and cook, stirring occasionally, for 5 minutes, or until softened.

2 Add the beef and cook, breaking it up with a wooden spoon, until browned all over. Stir in the celery and carrots and cook for 5 minutes. Season to taste with salt and pepper. Add the sugar, oregano and tomatoes. Bring to the boil, reduce the heat and simmer for 30 minutes.

3 Meanwhile, make the cheese sauce. Pour the milk into a saucepan and add the bay leaf, peppercorns, onion and mace. Heat gently to just below the boiling point, then remove from the heat, cover and leave to infuse for 10 minutes. Strain the milk into a jug. Melt the butter in a separate saucepan. Sprinkle in the flour and cook over a low heat, stirring constantly, for 1 minute. Remove from the heat and gradually stir in the warm milk. Return to the heat and bring to the boil, stirring. Cook, stirring, until thickened and smooth. Stir in the mustard and both cheeses, then season to taste with salt and pepper.

4 In a large, rectangular ovenproof dish, make alternate layers of meat sauce, lasagne and Parmesan cheese. Pour the cheese sauce over the layers, covering them completely, and sprinkle with Parmesan cheese. Bake in the preheated oven for 30 minutes, or until golden brown and bubbling. Serve immediately.

PIZZA MARGHERITA

SERVES 4
for the pizza dough
15 g/½ oz easy-blend dried yeast
1 tsp sugar
250 ml/9 fl oz warm water
350 g/12 oz strong white flour, plus
   extra for dusting
1 tsp salt
1 tbsp olive oil, plus extra for oiling

for the topping
400 g/14 oz canned chopped tomatoes
2 garlic cloves, crushed
2 tsp dried basil
1 tbsp olive oil
salt and pepper
2 tbsp tomato purée
100 g/3½ oz mozzarella cheese, chopped
2 tbsp freshly grated Parmesan cheese

GRANDMA'S TIPS

Nowadays pizza is served with all sorts of toppings – lots of them quite bizarre. This is a basic recipe that can be adapted to personal choice. Olives, both black and green, anchovy fillets, sliced mushrooms and salami all work well and add lots of colour and texture. Family members can make their own individual pizzas using their favourite toppings. Ready-made pizza bases are widely available and can be used when time is short.

1 Place the yeast and sugar in a measuring jug and mix with 50 ml/2 fl oz of the water. Leave the yeast mixture in a warm place for 15 minutes or until frothy.

2 Mix the flour with the salt and make a well in the centre. Add the oil, the yeast mixture and the remaining water. Using a wooden spoon, mix to form a smooth dough.

3 Turn the dough out onto a floured surface and knead for 4–5 minutes or until smooth.

4 Return the dough to the bowl, cover with an oiled sheet of clingfilm and leave to rise for 30 minutes or until doubled in size.

5 Knead the dough for 2 minutes. Stretch the dough with your hands, then place it on an oiled baking tray or pizza stone, pushing out the edges until even. The dough should be no more than 6 mm/¼ inch thick because it will rise during cooking.

6 Preheat the oven to 200°C/400°F/Gas Mark 6. To make the topping, place the tomatoes, garlic, dried basil, olive oil and salt and pepper to taste in a large frying pan and leave to simmer for 20 minutes or until the sauce has thickened. Stir in the tomato purée and leave to cool slightly.

7 Spread the topping evenly over the pizza base. Top with the mozzarella and Parmesan cheeses and bake in the preheated oven for 20–25 minutes. Serve hot.

RATATOUILLE

SERVES 4
2 aubergines
4 courgettes
2 yellow peppers
2 red peppers
2 onions

2 garlic cloves
150 ml/5 fl oz olive oil
1 bouquet garni
3 large tomatoes, peeled, deseeded and
   roughly chopped
salt and pepper

1 Roughly chop the aubergines and courgettes, and deseed and chop the peppers. Slice the onions and finely chop the garlic. Heat the oil in a large saucepan. Add the onions and cook over a low heat, stirring occasionally, for 5 minutes, or until softened. Add the garlic and cook, stirring frequently for a further 2 minutes.

2 Add the aubergines, courgettes and peppers. Increase the heat to medium and cook, stirring occasionally, until the peppers begin to colour. Add the bouquet garni, reduce the heat, cover and simmer gently for 40 minutes.

3 Stir in the chopped tomatoes and season to taste with salt and pepper. Re-cover the saucepan and simmer gently for a further 10 minutes. Remove and discard the bouquet garni. Serve warm or cold.

PAELLA

SERVES 4–6
1.2 litres/2 pints fish stock or water
12 large raw prawns, in their shells
½ tsp saffron threads
2 tbsp hot water
100 g/3½ oz skinless, boneless chicken
   breast, cut into ½-inch/1-cm pieces
100 g/3½ oz pork fillet, cut into ½-inch/
   1-cm pieces
salt and pepper
3 tbsp olive oil
100 g/3½ oz Spanish chorizo sausage,
   casing removed, cut into ½-inch/1-cm
   slices

1 large red onion, chopped
2 garlic cloves, crushed
½ tsp cayenne pepper
½ tsp paprika
1 red pepper, deseeded and sliced
1 green pepper, deseeded and sliced
12 cherry tomatoes, halved
350 g/12 oz medium-grain paella rice
1 tbsp chopped fresh parsley
2 tsp chopped fresh tarragon

GRANDMA'S TIPS

This traditional Spanish dish includes lots of ingredients, which is wonderful for a large party, but a simpler paella can be made using just chicken and prawns and would be great for everyday meals. Double the chicken and prawns in the recipe, and buy cooked prawns to save time. Follow the method, adding or omitting any vegetables as you wish.

1 Put the stock in a large pan and bring to a simmer. Add the prawns and cook for 2 minutes. Using a slotted spoon, transfer the prawns to a bowl and set aside. Let the stock simmer. Put the saffron threads and water in a small bowl or cup and let infuse for a few minutes.

2 Season the chicken and pork to taste with salt and pepper. Heat the oil in a paella pan or wide, shallow frying pan and cook the chicken, pork and chorizo over medium heat, stirring, for 5 minutes, or until golden. Add the onion and cook, stirring, for 2–3 minutes, or until softened. Add the garlic, cayenne pepper, paprika and saffron and its soaking liquid and cook, stirring constantly, for 1 minute. Add the pepper slices and tomato halves and cook, stirring, for a further 2 minutes.

3 Add the rice and herbs and cook, stirring constantly, for 1 minute, or until the rice is glossy and coated. Pour in all but 100 ml/3½ fl oz of the hot stock and bring to the boil. Reduce the heat and let simmer, uncovered, for 10 minutes. Do not stir during cooking, but shake the pan once or twice. Season to taste with salt and pepper, then shake the pan and cook for a further 10 minutes, or until the rice grains are plump and almost cooked. If the liquid is absorbed too quickly, pour in a little more hot stock, then shake the pan to spread the liquid through the paella. Do not stir it in. Add the prawns and shake the pan, but do not stir. Cook for a further 2 minutes.

4 When all the liquid has been absorbed and you detect a faint toasty aroma coming from the rice, remove from the heat immediately to prevent burning. Cover the pan with a clean tea towel or foil and let stand for 5 minutes. Divide the paella among warmed serving plates and serve immediately.

COQ AU VIN

SERVES 4
4 tbsp butter
2 tbsp olive oil
1.8 kg/4 lb chicken pieces
115 g/4 oz rindless smoked bacon,
  cut into strips
115 g/4 oz baby onions
115 g/4 oz chestnut mushrooms, halved

2 garlic cloves, finely chopped
2 tbsp brandy
225 ml/8 fl oz red wine
300 ml/10 fl oz chicken stock
1 bouquet garni
salt and pepper
2 tbsp plain flour
bay leaves, to garnish

GRANDMA'S TIPS

Coq au vin is usually made with red wine, but it also can be made with white wine like a Riesling. If you're using white wine, add 125 ml/4 fl oz of single cream before serving and garnish with freshly chopped parsley.

1 Melt half the butter with the olive oil in a large, flameproof casserole. Add the chicken and cook over a medium heat, stirring, for 8–10 minutes, or until golden brown all over. Add the bacon, onions, mushrooms and garlic.

2 Pour in the brandy and set it alight with a match or taper. When the flames have died down, add the wine, stock and bouquet garni and season to taste with salt and pepper. Bring to the boil, reduce the heat and simmer gently for 1 hour, or until the chicken pieces are cooked through and tender. Meanwhile, make a beurre manié by mashing the remaining butter with the flour in a small bowl.

3 Remove and discard the bouquet garni. Transfer the chicken to a large plate and keep warm. Stir the beurre manié into the casserole, a little at a time. Bring to the boil, return the chicken to the casserole and serve immediately, garnished with bay leaves.

BEEF BOURGUIGNON

SERVES 4–6

85 g/3 oz butter
2 tbsp sunflower oil
175 g/6 oz smoked lardons, blanched for
  30 seconds, drained and patted dry
900 g/2 lb braising beef, such as chuck
  or leg
2 large garlic cloves, crushed
1 carrot, diced
1 leek, halved and sliced
1 onion, finely chopped

2 tbsp plain flour
salt and pepper
350 ml/12 fl oz full-bodied red wine
about 500 ml/18 fl oz beef stock
1 tbsp tomato purée
1 bouquet garni
12 baby onions, peeled but kept whole
12 button mushrooms
chopped fresh flat-leaf parsley, to garnish
French bread, to serve

1 Preheat the oven to 150°C/300°F/Gas Mark 2. Heat 25 g/1 oz of the butter and 1 tablespoon of the oil in a large, flameproof casserole. Cook the lardons over a medium-high heat, stirring, for 2 minutes, or until beginning to brown. Using a slotted spoon, remove from the casserole and drain on kitchen paper.

2 Trim the beef and cut it into 5-cm/2-inch chunks. Add the beef to the casserole and cook over a high heat, stirring frequently, for 5 minutes, or until browned on all sides and sealed, adding more of the butter or oil to the casserole as necessary. Using a slotted spoon, transfer the beef to a plate.

3 Pour off all but 2 tablespoons of the fat from the casserole. Add the garlic, carrot, leek and onion and cook over a medium heat, stirring frequently, for 3 minutes, or until the onion is beginning to soften. Sprinkle in the flour, season to taste with salt and pepper, and cook, stirring constantly, for 2 minutes, then remove from the heat.

4 Gradually stir in the wine and stock and add the tomato purée and bouquet garni, then return to the heat and bring to the boil, stirring and scraping any sediment from the base of the casserole.

5 Return the beef and lardons to the casserole and add extra stock if necessary so that the ingredients are covered by about 1 cm/½ inch of liquid. Slowly return to the boil, then cover and cook in the preheated oven for 2 hours.

6 Meanwhile, heat 25 g/1 oz of the remaining butter and the remaining oil in a large sauté pan or frying pan and cook the baby onions over a medium-high heat, stirring frequently, until golden all over. Using a slotted spoon, transfer the onions to a plate.

7 Heat the remaining butter in the pan and cook the mushrooms, stirring frequently, until golden brown. Remove from the pan and then stir them, with the onions, into the casserole, re-cover and cook for a further 30 minutes, or until the beef is very tender.

8 Discard the bouquet garni, then adjust the seasoning to taste. Serve garnished with parsley, accompanied by plenty of French bread for mopping up all the juices.

CHILLI CON CARNE

SERVES 4
1 tbsp sunflower or corn oil
1 small onion, roughly chopped
1 or 2 garlic cloves, roughly chopped
1 green pepper, deseeded and diced
225 g/8 oz fresh beef mince
1 tsp chilli powder
400 g/14 oz canned chopped tomatoes

½ tsp salt (optional)
400 g/14 oz canned kidney beans,
  drained and rinsed

to serve
grated cheese
freshly cooked rice
tortilla chips

GRANDMA'S TIPS

*Always make sure you check the
strength of the chilli powder you
are using as it comes in different
strengths. If you don't like
your chilli too hot, use a mild
powder and decrease the amount.
Soured cream and guacamole are
traditional accompaniments.*

1 Heat the oil in a shallow frying pan over a low heat. Stir in the onion, garlic and green pepper and cook gently for 5 minutes.

2 Add the beef mince and stir well. Increase the heat to high and cook for 5 minutes, stirring occasionally. Spoon off any excess fat. Sprinkle over the chilli powder and mix well. Continue cooking for 2–3 minutes. Stir in the tomatoes, reduce the heat, cover and cook gently for at least 30 minutes. You may need to add a little water or beef stock if it starts to dry out.

3 Halfway through the cooking time check the seasoning and stir in the salt if needed. Add more chilli powder to taste, but be careful not to use too much.

4 Add the drained kidney beans to the chilli mixture 5–10 minutes before the end of the cooking time so that they heat through with the meat and spices.

5 Serve immediately topped with a little grated cheese and accompanied by freshly cooked rice and tortilla chips.

BEEF ENCHILADAS

MAKES 8
2 tbsp olive oil, plus extra for oiling
2 large onions, thinly sliced
550 g/1 lb 4 oz lean beef,
  cut into bite-size pieces
1 tbsp ground cumin
1–2 tsp cayenne pepper, or to taste
1 tsp paprika
salt and pepper
8 soft corn tortillas
1 quantity of bottled Taco Sauce,
  warmed and thinned with a little
  water if necessary
225 g/8 oz Cheddar cheese, grated

to serve
avocado, diced
red onion, finely chopped
mustard

GRANDMA'S TIPS
*These fun and colourful
enchiladas are great to have with
a group of friends. They can be
made with chicken as well as
beef so your friends can choose
which meat they prefer.*

1 Preheat the oven to 180°C/350°F/Gas Mark 4. Oil a large, rectangular baking dish.

2 Heat the oil in a large frying pan over a low heat. Add the onions and cook for 10 minutes, or until soft and golden. Remove with a slotted spoon and reserve.

3 Increase the heat to high, add the beef and cook, stirring, for 2–3 minutes, or until browned on all sides. Reduce the heat to medium, add the spices and salt and pepper to taste and cook, stirring constantly, for 2 minutes.

4 Warm each tortilla in a lightly oiled non-stick frying pan for 15 seconds on each side, then dip each, in turn, in the sauce. Top with a little of the beef, onions and grated cheese and roll up.

5 Place seam side down in the prepared baking dish, top with the remaining sauce and grated cheese and bake in the preheated oven for 30 minutes. Serve with the avocado, red onion and mustard.

CHICKEN TIKKA MASALA

SERVES 6
½ onion, roughly chopped
55 g/2 oz tomato purée
1 tsp cumin seeds
2.5-cm/1-inch piece fresh root ginger,
    chopped
3 tbsp lemon juice
2 garlic cloves, crushed
2 tsp chilli powder
750 g/1 lb 10 oz boneless chicken
salt and pepper
fresh mint sprigs, to garnish

for the masala sauce
2 tbsp ghee
1 onion, sliced
1 tbsp black onion seeds
3 garlic cloves, crushed
2 fresh green chillies, chopped
200 g/7 oz canned chopped tomatoes
125 ml/4 fl oz low-fat natural yogurt
125 ml/4 fl oz coconut milk
1 tbsp chopped fresh coriander
1 tbsp chopped fresh mint
2 tbsp lemon or lime juice
½ tsp garam masala

1 Combine the onion, tomato purée, cumin seeds, ginger, lemon juice, garlic and chilli powder in a food processor or blender and transfer to a bowl. Season to taste with salt and pepper. Cut chicken into 4-cm/1½-inch cubes. Stir into the bowl and leave for 2 hours.

2 Make the masala sauce. Heat the ghee in a saucepan, add the onion and stir over a medium heat for 5 minutes. Add the black onion seeds, garlic and chillies. Add the tomatoes, yogurt and coconut milk, bring to the boil, then simmer for 20 minutes.

3 Divide the chicken evenly between 8 oiled skewers and cook under a very hot preheated grill for 15 minutes, turning frequently. Remove the chicken and add to the sauce. Stir in the herbs, lemon juice and garam masala. Serve garnished with mint sprigs.

VEGETABLE KORMA

SERVES 4
4 tbsp ghee or vegetable oil
2 onions, chopped
2 garlic cloves, chopped
I fresh red chilli, chopped
I tbsp grated fresh root ginger
2 tomatoes, peeled and chopped
I orange pepper, deseeded and cut into
   small pieces
I large potato, cut into chunks
200 g/7 oz cauliflower florets

½ tsp salt
I tsp ground turmeric
I tsp ground cumin
I tsp ground coriander
I tsp garam masala
200 ml/7 fl oz vegetable stock or water
150 ml/5 fl oz natural yogurt
150 ml/5 fl oz single cream
25 g/I oz fresh coriander, chopped
freshly cooked rice, to serve

GRANDMA'S TIPS
*Try using other vegetables, such
as green beans, okra, carrots
and aubergines, to give a variety
of flavours and textures. If you
don't have all the spices just add
2 teaspoons of curry paste – or
more if you are feeling brave!*

1 Heat the ghee in a large saucepan over a medium heat, add the onions and garlic and
cook, stirring, for 3 minutes. Add the chilli and ginger and cook for a further 4 minutes.
Add the tomatoes, pepper, potato, cauliflower, salt and spices and cook, stirring, for a
further 3 minutes. Stir in the stock and bring to the boil. Reduce the heat and simmer
for 25 minutes.

2 Stir in the yogurt and cream and cook, stirring, for a further 5 minutes. Add the fresh
coriander and heat through.

3 Serve the curry with freshly cooked rice.

CHICKEN KIEV

SERVES 4
4 tbsp butter, softened
I garlic clove, finely chopped
I tbsp finely chopped fresh parsley
    plus extra sprigs to garnish
I tbsp finely chopped fresh oregano
salt and pepper
4 skinless, boneless chicken breasts
85 g/3 oz fresh white or wholemeal
    breadcrumbs

3 tbsp freshly grated Parmesan cheese
I egg, beaten
250 ml/9 fl oz vegetable oil, for
    deep-frying

to serve
freshly cooked new potatoes
selection of cooked vegetables

GRANDMA'S TIPS

Chill the herb butter well before using so that it won't melt too quickly during cooking. Sautéed sliced mushrooms or sun-dried tomatoes can be added to the butter for an interesting twist.

1 Place the butter and garlic in a bowl and mix together well. Stir in the chopped herbs and season well with salt and pepper. Pound the chicken breasts to flatten them to an even thickness, then place a tablespoon of herb butter in the centre of each one. Fold in the sides to enclose the butter, then secure with cocktail sticks.

2 Combine the breadcrumbs and grated Parmesan on a plate. Dip the chicken parcels into the beaten egg, then coat in the breadcrumb mixture. Transfer to a plate, cover and chill for 30 minutes. Remove from the refrigerator and coat in the egg and then the breadcrumb mixture for a second time.

3 Pour the oil into a deep-fat fryer to a depth that will cover the chicken parcels. Heat until it reaches 180–190°C/350–375°F, or until a cube of bread browns in 30 seconds. Transfer the chicken to the hot oil and deep-fry for 5 minutes, or until cooked through. Lift out the chicken and drain on kitchen paper.

4 Divide the chicken among 4 serving plates, garnish with parsley sprigs and serve with new potatoes and a selection of vegetables.

BEEF GOULASH

SERVES 4
2 tbsp vegetable oil
1 large onion, chopped
1 garlic clove, crushed
750 g/1 lb 10 oz lean braising beef
2 tbsp paprika
400 g/14 oz canned chopped tomatoes
2 tbsp tomato purée
1 large red pepper, deseeded and
  chopped

175 g/6 oz button mushrooms, sliced
600 ml/1 pint beef stock
1 tbsp cornflour
1 tbsp water
salt and pepper
chopped fresh parsley, to garnish
freshly cooked long-grain and wild rice,
  to serve

1 Heat the vegetable oil in a large, heavy-based frying pan. Add the onion and garlic and cook over a low heat for 3–4 minutes.

2 Using a sharp knife, cut the beef into chunks, add to the frying pan and cook over a high heat for 3 minutes, or until browned. Add the paprika and stir well, then add the tomatoes, tomato purée, red pepper and mushrooms. Cook for a further 2 minutes, stirring frequently. Pour in the stock. Bring to the boil, reduce the heat, cover and simmer for $1^1/_2$–2 hours, or until the meat is tender.

3 Blend the cornflour and water together in a small bowl, then add to the frying pan, stirring, until thickened and smooth. Cook for 1 minute. Season to taste with salt and pepper.

4 Transfer the beef goulash to a warmed serving dish, garnish with chopped fresh parsley and serve with a mix of long-grain and wild rice.

MUSHROOM
STROGANOFF

SERVES 4

550 g/1 lb 4 oz mixed fresh mushrooms,
  such as chanterelles, chestnut, ceps
  and oyster
1 red onion, diced
2 garlic cloves, crushed
425 ml/15 fl oz vegetable stock
1 tbsp tomato purée

2 tbsp lemon juice
15 g/½ oz cornflour
2 tbsp cold water
115 g/4 oz low-fat natural yogurt
3 tbsp chopped fresh parsley
freshly ground black pepper
freshly cooked brown or white rice,
  to serve

GRANDMA'S TIPS

*This is a vegetarian version of
the traditional beef stroganoff.
Extra soured cream and a dash
of paprika make a colourful
and tasty garnish.*

1 Put the mushrooms, onion, garlic, stock, tomato purée and lemon juice into a saucepan and bring to the boil. Reduce the heat, cover and simmer for 15 minutes, or until the onion is tender.

2 Blend the cornflour with the water in a small bowl and stir into the mushroom mixture. Return to the boil, stirring constantly, and cook until the sauce thickens. Reduce the heat and simmer for a further 2–3 minutes, stirring occasionally.

3 Just before serving, remove the saucepan from the heat and stir in the yogurt, making sure that the stroganoff is not boiling or it may separate and curdle. Stir in 2 tablespoons of the parsley and season to taste with pepper. Transfer the stroganoff to a warmed serving dish, sprinkle over the remaining parsley and serve immediately with freshly cooked brown or white rice.

SWEET & SOUR
PRAWNS

SERVES 4
450 g/1 lb cooked tiger prawns
1 tbsp groundnut or sunflower oil
4 spring onions, finely chopped
2 tsp finely chopped fresh root ginger
2 tbsp dark soy sauce
2 tbsp muscovado sugar
3 tbsp rice vinegar

1 tbsp Chinese rice wine
125 ml/4 fl oz fish or chicken stock
1 tsp cornflour
1–2 tbsp water
dash of sesame oil
shredded Chinese leaves, to serve
shredded spring onion, to garnish

GRANDMA'S TIPS

For a change, try making this dish with pork fillet instead of prawns. Finely slice the pork into medallions and fry in the wok or large frying pan, turning occasionally until cooked through. Then add the other ingredients as the recipe directs.

1 Peel and devein the prawns, pat dry with kitchen paper and reserve.

2 Heat the oil in a preheated wok or large frying pan. Add the spring onions and ginger and stir-fry over a high heat for 1 minute. Add the soy sauce, sugar, vinegar, rice wine and stock and bring to the boil.

3 Place the cornflour and water in a small bowl and mix to make a paste. Stir 1 tablespoon of the paste into the sauce and add the prawns. Cook, stirring, until slightly thickened and smooth. Sprinkle with sesame oil.

4 Make a bed of Chinese leaves in 4 serving bowls and top with prawns and sauce. Garnish with the shredded spring onion and serve immediately.

PORK CHOW MEIN

SERVES 4

250 g/9 oz egg noodles
4–5 tbsp vegetable oil
250 g/9 oz pork fillet, cooked
125g/4 ½ oz French beans
2 tbsp light soy sauce

1 tsp salt
½ tsp sugar
1 tbsp Chinese rice wine or dry sherry
2 spring onions, finely shredded
a few drops sesame oil
chilli sauce, to serve (optional)

1 Cook the noodles in boiling water according to the instructions on the packet, then drain and rinse under cold water. Drain again then toss with 1 tablespoon of the oil.

2 Slice the pork into thin shreds and trim the beans.

3 Heat 3 tablespoons of the oil in a preheated wok until hot. Add the noodles and stir-fry for 2–3 minutes with 1 tablespoon of the soy sauce, then remove to a serving dish. Keep warm.

4 Heat the remaining oil and stir-fry the beans and meat for 2 minutes. Add the salt, sugar, rice wine, the remaining soy sauce and about half of the spring onions to the wok.

5 Stir the mixture in the wok, adding a little stock if necessary, then pour on top of the noodles, and sprinkle with sesame oil and the remaining spring onions.

6 Serve the chow mein hot or cold with chilli sauce, if using.

SPICY BEEF WITH
BLACK BEAN SAUCE

SERVES 2

2 tbsp groundnut or vegetable oil
2 onions, cut into wedges
2 garlic cloves, finely chopped
1 tsp pepper
450 g/1 lb beef fillet, cut into thick strips
55 g/2 oz baby sweetcorn,
   halved lengthways

115 g/4 oz shiitake mushrooms,
   thickly sliced
6 tbsp soy sauce
125 g/4½ oz black bean sauce
1 tsp palm sugar
chopped fresh coriander, to garnish
cooked medium egg noodles, to serve

GRANDMA'S TIPS

If you prefer more sauce with the beef, use extra sauce with a little water. Don't stir-fry the vegetable for too long to keep their crunch.

1 Heat the oil in a preheated wok, add the onions and stir-fry over a medium–high heat for 2–3 minutes until starting to soften.

2 Add the garlic and pepper and stir well, then add the beef strips, baby sweetcorn and mushrooms and stir-fry over a high heat for 2–3 minutes. Add half the soy sauce, the black bean sauce and sugar and stir-fry for 1–2 minutes.

3 Serve immediately with egg noodles, tossed in the remaining soy sauce, garnished with chopped coriander.

Christmas and other holidays were always when Grandma came into her own. She would love having her family around her and always pulled out all the stops to give them the best of everything. Starters of special soups and pâté are included in this chapter and there are, of course, recipes for roast turkey and the all-important stuffing. Gammon, goose and beef wellington recipes are also provided as alternatives to the turkey but they are just as good for winter dinners – and the salmon dish is ideal for a summer's day too.

GRANDMA'S FESTIVE FARE

Vegetarians are not forgotten as there is a mixed nut roast to be served with a cranberry and red wine sauce, and some delicious individual vegetable dishes too. Those with a sweet tooth will not be disappointed either, as there are two very special desserts to choose from – either the customary Christmas pudding or a festive sherry trifle. These recipes can be used at other times of the year to celebrate any festival in the calendar or special family event, like a birth, christening or birthday.

WILD MUSHROOM & SHERRY SOUP

SERVES 4
2 tbsp olive oil
1 onion, chopped
1 garlic clove, chopped
125 g/4½ oz sweet potato, peeled and chopped
1 leek, trimmed and sliced
200 g/7 oz chestnut mushrooms
150 g/5½ oz mixed wild mushrooms

600 ml/1 pint vegetable stock
350 ml/12 fl oz single cream
4 tbsp sherry
salt and pepper

to garnish/serve
Parmesan cheese shavings
sautéed sliced wild mushrooms
fresh crusty bread

GRANDMA'S TIPS

When you can only find cultivated mushrooms, increase the flavour of the dish by adding some dried porcini mushrooms. Rehydrate the porcini in a little hot water to cover for 15–20 minutes and then add both the porcini and their soaking liquid to the soup.

1 Heat the oil in a saucepan over a medium heat. Add the onion and garlic and cook, stirring, for 3 minutes until softened slightly. Add the sweet potato and cook for another 3 minutes. Stir in the leek and cook for another 2 minutes.

2 Stir in the mushrooms, stock and cream. Bring to the boil, then reduce the heat and simmer gently, stirring occasionally, for about 25 minutes. Remove from the heat, stir in the sherry, and leave to cool a little.

3 Transfer half of the soup into a food processor and blend until smooth. Return the mixture to the pan with the rest of the soup, season with salt and pepper and reheat gently, stirring. Pour into 4 warmed soup bowls, garnish with Parmesan shavings and sautéed wild mushrooms, and serve with fresh crusty bread.

CREAMY CARROT &
PARSNIP SOUP

SERVES 4
4 tbsp butter
1 large onion, chopped
450 g/1 lb carrots, chopped
2 large parsnips, chopped
1 tbsp grated fresh root ginger

1 tsp grated orange rind
600 ml/1 pint vegetable stock
125 ml/4 fl oz single cream
salt and pepper
sprigs of fresh coriander, to garnish

GRANDMA'S TIPS

These two vegetables are a great combination giving a rich and delicious heart-warming soup. But if you prefer one more than the other, add more of one and less of the other.

1 Melt the butter in a large saucepan over a low heat. Add the onion and cook, stirring, for 3 minutes, until slightly softened. Add the carrots and parsnips, cover the pan and cook, stirring occasionally, for about 15 minutes, until the vegetables have softened a little. Stir in the ginger, orange rind and stock. Bring to the boil, then reduce the heat, cover the pan and simmer for 30–35 minutes, until the vegetables are tender. Remove from the heat and leave to cool for 10 minutes.

2 Transfer the soup to a food processor or blender and process until smooth. Return the soup to the rinsed-out saucepan, stir in the cream and season well with salt and pepper. Warm through gently over a low heat.

3 Remove from the heat and ladle into soup bowls. Garnish each bowl with pepper and a sprig of coriander and serve.

CHICKEN LIVER PÂTÉ

SERVES 4–6
200 g/7 oz butter
225 g/8 oz trimmed chicken livers,
  thawed if frozen
2 tbsp Marsala or brandy
1½ tsp chopped fresh sage

1 garlic clove, coarsely chopped
150 ml/5 fl oz double cream
salt and pepper
fresh bay leaves or sage leaves,
  to garnish
crackers, to serve

1 Melt 40 g/1½ oz of the butter in a large, heavy-based frying pan. Add the chicken livers and cook over a medium heat for about 4 minutes on each side. They should be browned on the outside but still pink in the middle. Transfer to a food processor and process until finely chopped.

2 Stir the Marsala or brandy into the pan, scraping up any sediment with a wooden spoon, then add to the food processor with the chopped sage, garlic and 100 g/3½ oz of the remaining butter. Process until smooth. Add the cream, season with salt and pepper and process until thoroughly combined and smooth. Spoon the pâté into a dish or individual ramekins, smooth the surface and leave to cool completely.

3 Melt the remaining butter, then spoon it over the surface of the pâté. Decorate with herb leaves, cool, then chill in the refrigerator. Serve with crackers.

CHESTNUT, MADEIRA & MUSHROOM TARTS

MAKES 12
pastry
100 g/3½ oz unsalted butter, chilled and
  diced, plus extra for greasing
225 g/8 oz plain flour, plus extra for
  dusting
pinch of salt

filling
25 g/1 oz unsalted butter
1 tsp olive oil
1 shallot, finely chopped

1 garlic clove, crushed
8 cooked chestnuts, peeled and
  roughly chopped
200 g/7 oz chestnut mushrooms,
  chopped
2 tbsp Madeira
150 ml/5 fl oz double cream
1 egg, plus 1 egg yolk
salt and pepper
chopped fresh parsley, to serve

GRANDMA'S TIPS

*These cheeky little pastries do
not have to be served only at
Christmas time. They are ideal
for dinner parties as a starter or
can form part of a party food
spread.*

1 Lightly grease a 7.5-cm/3-inch, 12-hole muffin tin with butter. Sift the flour into a
large bowl, add the salt and rub in the remaining butter until the mixture resembles
breadcrumbs. Add a little cold water – just enough to bring the dough together. Knead
the dough briefly on a floured work surface.

2 Divide the pastry in half. Roll out 1 piece of pastry and, using a 9-cm/3½-inch plain
pastry cutter, cut out 6 rounds, then roll each round into a 12-cm/4½-inch round.
Repeat with the remaining pastry until you have 12 rounds of pastry, then use to line the
muffin tin. Chill in the refrigerator for 30 minutes.

3 Meanwhile, preheat the oven to 200°C/400°F/Gas Mark 6 and make the filling. Melt
the butter with the oil in a small frying pan over a low heat, add the shallot and garlic and
cook, stirring occasionally, for 5–8 minutes until the shallot is transparent and soft. Add
the chestnuts and mushrooms and cook, stirring, for 2 minutes, then add the Madeira
and simmer for 2 minutes.

4 Line the pastry cases with baking paper and fill with baking beans, then bake in the
preheated oven for 10 minutes. Carefully lift out the paper and beans, and reduce the
oven temperature to 190°C/375°F/Gas Mark 5. Stir the cream, whole egg and egg
yolk into the mushroom mixture and season well with salt and pepper. Divide between
the pastry cases and bake for 10 minutes. Leave to cool in the tin for 5 minutes, then
carefully remove from the tin, scatter with chopped parsley and serve.

SMOKED SALMON, DILL & HORSERADISH TARTLETS

MAKES 6

for the pastry
125 g/4½ oz plain flour, plus extra for
   dusting
pinch of salt
75 g/2½ oz cold butter, cut into pieces,
   plus extra for greasing
cold water

for the filling
125 ml/4 fl oz crème fraîche
1 tsp creamed horseradish
½ tsp lemon juice
1 tsp Spanish capers, chopped
salt and pepper
3 egg yolks
200 g/7 oz smoked salmon trimmings
bunch fresh dill, chopped, plus extra
   sprigs to garnish

GRANDMA'S TIPS

*If you're short of time, you
can use ready-made shortcrust
pastry to make the tartlets or
you can use ready-made tartlet
cases instead. The filling can
also be used to make one larger
(20-cm/8-inch) tart if you
prefer – just increase the baking
time to 20–25 minutes.*

1 Butter six 9-cm/3½-inch loose-bottomed fluted tart tins. Sift the flour and salt into a food processor, add the butter and process until the mixture resembles fine breadcrumbs. Tip the mixture into a large bowl and add a little cold water, just enough to bring the dough together. Turn out on to a floured surface and divide into 6 equal-sized pieces. Roll each piece to fit the tart tins. Carefully fit each piece of pastry in its case and press well to fit the tin. Roll the rolling pin over the tin to neaten the edges and trim the excess pastry. Cut 6 pieces of baking paper and fit a piece into each tartlet, fill with baking beans and chill in the refrigerator for 30 minutes. Meanwhile, preheat the oven to 200°C/400°F/Gas Mark 6.

2 Bake the tart cases blind for 10 minutes in the preheated oven then remove the beans and baking paper.

3 Meanwhile, put the crème fraîche, horseradish, lemon juice, capers and salt and pepper into a bowl and mix well. Add the egg yolks, the smoked salmon and the dill and carefully mix again. Divide this mixture among the tartlet cases and return to the oven for 10 minutes. Cool in the tins for 5 minutes before serving garnished with dill sprigs.

ROAST TURKEY
WITH STUFFING

SERVES 8
1 x 5-kg/11-lb turkey
55 g/2 oz butter
5 tbsp red wine
400 ml/14 fl oz chicken stock
1 tbsp cornflour
1 tsp French mustard
1 tsp sherry vinegar

for the stuffing
225 g/8 oz pork sausagemeat
225 g/8 oz unsweetened chestnut purée
85 g/3 oz walnuts
115 g/4 oz dried apricots, chopped
2 tbsp chopped fresh parsley
2 tbsp chopped fresh chives
2 tsp chopped fresh sage
4–5 tbsp double cream
salt and pepper

1 To make the stuffing, combine the sausagemeat and chestnut purée in a bowl, then stir in the walnuts, apricots, parsley, chives and sage. Stir in enough cream to make a firm, but not dry, mixture. Season with salt and pepper.

2 Preheat the oven to 220°C/425°F/Gas Mark 7. If you are planning to stuff the turkey, fill only the neck cavity and close the flap of skin with a skewer. Alternatively, the stuffing may be cooked separately, either rolled into small balls or spooned into an ovenproof dish, for the last 30–40 minutes of the cooking time.

3 Place the bird in a large roasting tin and rub all over with 40 g/1½ oz of the butter. Roast for 1 hour, then lower the oven temperature to 180°C/350°F/Gas Mark 4 and roast for an additional 2½ hours. You may need to pour off the fat from the roasting tin occasionally.

4 Check that the turkey is cooked by inserting a skewer or the point of a sharp knife into the thigh; if the juices run clear, it is ready. Transfer the bird to a carving board, cover loosely with foil, and let rest.

5 To make the gravy, skim off the fat from the roasting tin then place the pan over a medium heat. Add the red wine and stir with a wooden spoon, scraping up the sediment from the bottom of the pan. Stir in the chicken stock. Mix the cornflour, mustard, vinegar, and 2 teaspoons of water together in a small bowl, then stir into the wine and stock. Bring to the boil, stirring constantly until thickened and smooth. Stir in the remaining butter.

6 Carve the turkey and serve with the stuffing and gravy.

YULETIDE GOOSE
WITH HONEY & PEARS

SERVES 4

1 x oven-ready goose, weighing
   3.5–4.5 kg/7 lb 12 oz–10 lb
1 tsp salt
4 pears

1 tbsp lemon juice
55 g/2 oz butter
2 tbsp clear honey
seasonal vegetables, to serve

GRANDMA'S TIPS

When the goose is cooking, pour off the fat every 20 minutes and reserve. Strain and pour into clean preserving jars. It will keep in the fridge for up to a year. Goose fat makes the best-ever roast potatoes.

1 Preheat the oven to 220°C/425°F/Gas Mark 7.

2 Rinse the goose and pat dry. Use a fork to prick the skin all over, then rub with the salt. Place the bird upside down on a rack in a roasting tin. Roast in the oven for 30 minutes. Drain off the fat. Turn the bird over and roast for 15 minutes. Drain off the fat. Reduce the temperature to 180°C/350°F/Gas Mark 4 and roast for 15 minutes per 450 g/1 lb. Cover with foil 15 minutes before the end of the cooking time. Check that the bird is cooked by inserting a knife between the legs and body. If the juices run clear, it is cooked. Remove from the oven.

3 Peel and halve the pears and brush with lemon juice. Melt the butter and honey in a saucepan over a low heat, then add the pears. Cook, stirring, for 5–10 minutes until tender. Remove from the heat, arrange the pears around the goose and pour the sweet juices over the bird. Serve with seasonal vegetables.

GLAZED GAMMON

SERVES 8

1 x 4-kg/9-lb gammon
1 apple, cored and chopped
1 onion, chopped
300 ml/10 fl oz cider

6 black peppercorns
1 bouquet garni
1 bay leaf
about 50 cloves
4 tbsp demerara sugar

GRANDMA'S TIPS

*After removing the rind from
the gammon, try spreading
2 tablespoons of mustard over
the fat to give the ham some
extra flavour, then score the fat
into a diamond-shaped pattern
and stud with the cloves.*

1 Put the gammon in a large saucepan and add enough cold water to cover. Bring to the boil and skim off the scum that rises to the surface. Reduce the heat and simmer for 30 minutes. Drain the gammon and return to the saucepan. Add the apple, onion, cider, peppercorns, bouquet garni, bay leaf and a few of the cloves. Pour in enough fresh water to cover and bring back to the boil. Cover and simmer for 3 hours 20 minutes.

2 Preheat the oven to 200°C/400°F/Gas Mark 6. Take the saucepan off the heat and set aside to cool slightly. Remove the gammon from the cooking liquid and, while it is still warm, loosen the rind with a sharp knife, then peel it off and discard. Score the fat into diamond shapes and stud with the remaining cloves. Place the gammon on a rack in a roasting tin and sprinkle with the sugar. Roast, basting occasionally with the cooking liquid, for 20 minutes. Serve hot or cold.

FESTIVE BEEF
WELLINGTON

SERVES 4
750 g/1 lb 10 oz thick beef fillet
2 tbsp butter
salt and pepper
2 tbsp vegetable oil
1 garlic clove, chopped

1 onion, chopped
175 g/6 oz chestnut mushrooms
1 tbsp chopped fresh sage
350 g/12 oz frozen puff pastry, defrosted
1 egg, beaten

1 Preheat the oven to 220°C/425°F/Gas Mark 7. Put the beef in a roasting tin, spread with butter and season with salt and pepper. Roast for 30 minutes, then remove from the oven. Meanwhile, heat the oil in a pan over a medium heat. Add the garlic and onion and cook, stirring, for 3 minutes. Stir in the mushrooms, sage and salt and pepper to taste and cook for 5 minutes. Remove from the heat.

2 Roll out the pastry into a rectangle large enough to enclose the beef, then place the beef in the middle and spread the mushroom mixture over it. Bring the long sides of the pastry together over the beef and seal with beaten egg. Tuck the short ends over (trim away excess pastry) and seal. Place on a baking sheet, seam-side down. Make 2 slits in the top. Decorate with dough shapes and brush with beaten egg. Bake for 40 minutes. If the pastry browns too quickly, cover with foil. Remove from the oven, cut into thick slices and serve hot.

RACK OF LAMB

SERVES 2
1 trimmed rack of lamb, weighing
  250–300 g/9–10½ oz
1 garlic clove, crushed
150 ml/5 fl oz red wine
1 fresh rosemary sprig, crushed to
  release the flavour
salt and pepper
1 tbsp olive oil
150 ml/5 fl oz lamb stock
2 tbsp redcurrant jelly

for the mint sauce
bunch fresh mint leaves
2 tsp caster sugar
2 tbsp boiling water
2 tbsp white wine vinegar

GRANDMA'S TIPS

This is an ideal roast to make for just two people. For more, double or treble the quantity. It makes a very good dinner party dish and is easy to carve. Serve with a mixture of spring vegetables and garnish with rosemary.

1 Place the rack of lamb in a non-metallic bowl and rub all over with the garlic. Pour over the wine and place the rosemary sprig on top. Cover and leave to marinate in the refrigerator for 3 hours or overnight if possible.

2 Preheat the oven to 220°C/425°F/Gas Mark 7. Remove the lamb from the marinade, reserving the marinade. Pat the meat dry with kitchen paper and season well with salt and pepper. Place it in a small roasting tin, drizzle with the oil and roast for 15–20 minutes, depending on whether you like your meat pink or medium. Remove the lamb from the oven and leave to rest, covered with foil, in a warm place for 5 minutes.

3 Meanwhile, pour the reserved marinade into a small saucepan, bring to the boil over a medium heat and boil rapidly for 5 minutes. Add the stock and redcurrant jelly and simmer, stirring, until the mixture is syrupy.

4 To make the mint sauce, chop the fresh mint leaves and mix together with the sugar in a small bowl. Add the boiling water and stir to dissolve the sugar. Add the white wine vinegar and leave to stand for 30 minutes before serving with the lamb.

5 Carve the lamb into cutlets and serve on warmed plates with the sauce spooned over the top. Serve the mint sauce separately.

POACHED SALMON

SERVES 8–12
4 litres/7 pints water
6 tbsp white wine vinegar
1 large onion, sliced
2 carrots, sliced
1½ tbsp salt

1 tsp black peppercorns
one 2.7-kg/6-lb .salmon, cleaned,
 with gills and eyes removed
fresh dill, to garnish
salad, to serve

GRANDMA'S TIPS

This is a great dish for a big dinner party. If you have guests who prefer a warmer option, melt some butter, add some extra dill, and serve with the fish.

1 To make a court-bouillon (stock) in which to poach the fish, put the water, vinegar, onion, carrots, salt and peppercorns in a large fish kettle or covered roasting tin and bring to the boil. Reduce the heat and simmer for 20 minutes. Remove the trivet (if using a fish kettle) and lay the salmon on it. Lower it into the court-bouillon, cover, return to simmering point and cook for 5 minutes. Turn off the heat and leave the fish, covered, to cool in the liquid.

2 When the fish is cold, lift it out of the kettle on the trivet and drain well. Using 2 fish slices, carefully transfer to a board. Using a sharp knife, remove the head, then slit the skin along the backbone and peel off. Carefully turn the fish over and peel off the skin on the other side.

3 Garnish with dill and serve with salad.

MIXED NUT ROAST WITH CRANBERRY & RED WINE SAUCE

SERVES 4

2 tbsp butter, plus extra for greasing
2 garlic cloves, chopped
1 large onion, chopped
50 g/1¾ oz pine kernels, toasted
75 g/2¾ oz hazelnuts, toasted
50 g/1¾ oz walnuts, ground
50 g/1¾ oz cashew nuts, ground
100 g/3½ oz wholemeal breadcrumbs
1 egg, lightly beaten

2 tbsp chopped fresh thyme
250 ml/9 fl oz vegetable stock
salt and pepper
sprigs of fresh thyme, to garnish

for the cranberry & red wine sauce
175 g/6 oz fresh cranberries
100 g/3½ oz caster sugar
300 ml/10 fl oz red wine
1 cinnamon stick

1 Preheat the oven to 180°C/350°F/Gas Mark 4. Grease a loaf tin and line it with greaseproof paper. Melt the butter in a saucepan over a medium heat. Add the garlic and onion and cook, stirring, for about 3 minutes. Remove the pan from the heat. Grind the pine kernels and hazelnuts. Stir all the nuts into the pan and add the breadcrumbs, egg, thyme, stock and seasoning.

2 Spoon the mixture into the loaf tin and level the surface. Cook in the centre of the preheated oven for 30 minutes or until cooked through and golden. The loaf is cooked when a skewer inserted into the centre comes out clean. Halfway through the cooking time, make the cranberry and red wine sauce. Put all the ingredients in a saucepan and bring to the boil. Reduce the heat and simmer, stirring occasionally, for 15 minutes.

3 Remove the nut roast from the oven and turn out. Garnish with sprigs of thyme and serve with the cranberry and red wine sauce.

PERFECT ROAST
POTATOES

SERVES 6
1.3 kg/3 lb large floury potatoes, such as
    King Edward, Maris Piper or Desirée,
    peeled and cut into even-sized chunks
salt
3 tbsp goose fat, duck fat or olive oil

GRANDMA'S TIPS

*The potatoes can be seasoned
while they're roasting, which
allows the flavours to be
absorbed. Parsnips can also be
roasted in the same way but
they'll only need 2–3 minutes'
precooking and they don't need
to be shaken in the pan.*

1 Preheat the oven to 220°C/425°F/Gas Mark 7.

2 Cook the potatoes in a large saucepan of lightly salted boiling water over a medium heat, covered, for 5–7 minutes. They will still be firm. Remove from the heat. Meanwhile, add the fat to a roasting tin and place in the hot oven.

3 Drain the potatoes well and return them to the saucepan. Cover with the lid and firmly shake the pan so that the surface of the potatoes is slightly roughened to help give a much crisper texture.

4 Remove the roasting tin from the oven and carefully tip the potatoes into the hot fat. Baste them to ensure that they are all coated with it.

5 Roast the potatoes at the top of the oven for 45–50 minutes until they are browned all over and thoroughly crisp. Turn the potatoes and baste again only once during the process or the crunchy edges will be destroyed.

6 Using a slotted spoon, carefully transfer the potatoes from the roasting tin into a warmed serving dish. Sprinkle with a little salt and serve immediately. Any leftovers (although this is most unlikely) are delicious cold.

GLAZED TURNIPS

SERVES 4–6
900 g/2 lb young turnips, peeled and
    quartered
salt and pepper
55 g/2 oz butter

I tbsp brown sugar
150 ml/5 fl oz vegetable stock
I sprig of fresh rosemary
chopped fresh parsley and grated orange
    rind, to garnish

GRANDMA'S TIPS

*As a variation, cook the turnips
in a saucepan of boiling water
for 20–25 minutes, or until
tender. Drain well. Place the
juice and grated rind of 1 orange
and 1 tablespoon of honey in the
rinsed-out saucepan and reduce
until thick. Add the cooked
turnips and toss to glaze. This
dish is particularly delicious
served with duck.*

1 Put the turnips into a saucepan of boiling salted water, bring back to the boil and
simmer for 10 minutes. Drain well.

2 Melt the butter in the rinsed-out saucepan over a gentle heat, add the turnips and
sugar and mix to coat well.

3 Add the stock with the rosemary and bring to the boil. Reduce the heat and simmer
for 15–20 minutes with the lid off the pan so that the juices reduce and the turnips are
tender and well glazed.

4 Remove the pan from the heat, discard the rosemary and season with salt and pepper
to taste.

5 Serve immediately garnished with the chopped parsley and grated orange rind.

ROASTED ROOT VEGETABLES

SERVES 4–6

3 parsnips, cut into 5-cm/2-inch chunks
4 baby turnips, quartered
3 carrots, cut into 5-cm/2-inch chunks
450 g/1 lb butternut squash, peeled and cut into 5-cm/2-inch chunks
450 g/1 lb sweet potatoes, peeled and cut into 5-cm/2-inch chunks

2 garlic cloves, finely chopped
2 tbsp chopped fresh rosemary
2 tbsp chopped fresh thyme
2 tsp chopped fresh sage
3 tbsp olive oil
salt and pepper
2 tbsp chopped fresh mixed herbs, such as parsley, thyme and mint, to garnish

1 Preheat the oven to 220°C/425°F/Gas Mark 7.

2 Arrange all the vegetables in a single layer in a large roasting tin. Scatter over the garlic and the herbs. Pour over the oil and season well with salt and pepper.

3 Toss all the ingredients together until they are well mixed and coated with the oil (you can leave them to marinate at this stage to allow the flavours to be absorbed).

4 Roast the vegetables at the top of the oven for 50–60 minutes until they are cooked and nicely browned. Turn the vegetables over halfway through the cooking time.

5 Serve with a good handful of fresh herbs scattered on top and a final sprinkling of salt and pepper to taste.

HONEYED PARSNIPS

SERVES 4
8 parsnips, peeled and quartered
4 tbsp vegetable oil
1 tbsp honey

GRANDMA'S TIPS

For a change try substituting maple syrup for the honey or use a mixture of root vegetables for a colourful dish.

1 Preheat the oven to 180°C/350°F/Gas Mark 4.

2 Bring a large saucepan of water to the boil. Reduce the heat, add the parsnips and cook for 5 minutes. Drain thoroughly.

3 Pour 2 tablespoons of the oil into a shallow, ovenproof dish and add the parsnips. Mix the remaining oil with the honey and drizzle over the parsnips. Roast in the preheated oven for 45 minutes until golden brown and tender. Remove from the oven and serve.

BRUSSELS SPROUTS WITH BUTTERED CHESTNUTS

SERVES 4
350 g/12 oz Brussels sprouts, trimmed
3 tbsp butter
100 g/3½ oz canned whole chestnuts

pinch of nutmeg
salt and pepper
50 g/1¾ oz flaked almonds, to garnish

GRANDMA'S TIPS
Take care when buying canned chestnuts not to buy the sweetened ones. Instead of canned chestnuts, try vacuum packed ones, which are easy to find and use. Dried chestnuts are available from health food shops but they'll need a good soaking, preferably overnight, before use.

1 Bring a large saucepan of water to the boil. Add the Brussels sprouts and cook for 5 minutes. Drain thoroughly.

2 Melt the butter in a large saucepan over a medium heat. Add the Brussels sprouts and cook, stirring, for 3 minutes, then add the chestnuts and nutmeg. Season with salt and pepper and stir well. Cook for another 2 minutes, stirring, then remove from the heat. Transfer to a serving dish, scatter over the almonds and serve.

BRANDY SNAPS

MAKES ABOUT 20
85 g/3 oz unsalted butter
85 g/3 oz golden caster sugar
3 tbsp golden syrup
85 g/3 oz plain flour
1 tsp ground ginger
1 tbsp brandy
finely grated rind of ½ lemon

filling
150 ml/5 fl oz double cream
  or whipping cream
1 tbsp brandy (optional)
1 tbsp icing sugar

1 Preheat the oven to 160°C/325°F/Gas Mark 3. Line three large baking trays with baking paper.

2 Place the butter, sugar and golden syrup in a saucepan and heat gently over a low heat, stirring occasionally, until melted. Remove from the heat and leave to cool slightly. Sift the flour and ginger into the pan and beat until smooth, then stir in the brandy and lemon rind.

3 Drop small spoonfuls of the mixture onto the prepared baking trays, leaving plenty of room for spreading. Place one baking tray at a time in the preheated oven for 10–12 minutes, or until the snaps are golden brown.

4 Remove the first baking tray from the oven and leave to cool for about 30 seconds, then lift each round with a palette knife and wrap around the handle of a wooden spoon. If the brandy snaps start to become too firm to wrap, return them to the oven for about 30 seconds to soften again. When firm, remove from the spoon handles and finish cooling on a wire rack. Repeat with the remaining baking trays.

5 For the filling, whip the cream with the brandy and icing sugar until thick. Just before serving, pipe the cream mixture into each end of the brandy snaps.

CHRISTMAS PUDDING

SERVES 4
200 g/7 oz currants
200 g/7 oz raisins
200 g/7 oz sultanas
150 ml/5 fl oz sweet sherry
175 g/6 oz butter, plus extra for greasing
175 g/6 oz brown sugar
4 eggs, beaten
150 g/5½ oz self-raising flour

100 g/3½ oz fresh white or wholemeal
  breadcrumbs
50 g/1¾ oz blanched almonds, chopped
juice of 1 orange
grated rind of ½ orange
grated rind of ½ lemon
½ tsp ground mixed spice
holly leaves, to decorate

GRANDMA'S TIPS
Leftover Christmas pudding makes a lovely dessert when cut into small portions and quickly fried in a little butter. Serve hot with some ice cream.

1 Put the currants, raisins and sultanas into a glass bowl and pour over the sherry. Leave to soak for at least 2 hours.

2 Mix the butter and sugar in a bowl. Beat in the eggs, then fold in the flour. Stir in the soaked fruit and sherry with the breadcrumbs, almonds, orange juice and rind, lemon rind and mixed spice. Grease a pudding basin and press the mixture into it, leaving a gap of 2.5 cm/1 inch at the top. Cut a circle of greaseproof paper 3 cm/1¼ inches larger than the top of the basin, grease with butter and place over the pudding. Secure with string, then top with 2 layers of foil. Place the pudding in a pan filled with boiling water which reaches two-thirds of the way up the basin. Reduce the heat and simmer for 6 hours, topping up with boiling water when necessary.

3 Remove from the heat and leave to cool. Renew the greaseproof paper and foil and refrigerate for 2–8 weeks. To reheat, steam for 2 hours as before. Decorate with holly and serve.

FESTIVE SHERRY TRIFLE

SERVES 8
for the fruit layer
100 g/3½ oz trifle sponges
150 ml/5 fl oz strawberry jam
250 ml/9 fl oz sherry
150 g/5½ oz fresh strawberries, hulled
  and sliced
400 g/14 oz canned mixed fruit, drained
1 large banana, sliced

for the custard layer
6 egg yolks
50 g/1¾ oz caster sugar
500 ml/18 fl oz milk
1 tsp vanilla essence

for the topping
300 ml/10 fl oz double cream
1–2 tbsp caster sugar
chocolate curls or flakes, to decorate

GRANDMA'S TIPS
Instead of trifle sponges, you could use macaroon biscuits, sponge fingers or even sliced Swiss roll. For an even more exotic flavour, try substituting Cassis or Framboise liqueur for the sherry.

1 Spread the trifle sponges with jam, cut them into bite-sized cubes and arrange in the bottom of a large glass serving bowl. Pour over the sherry and leave for 30 minutes.

2 Combine the strawberries, canned fruit and banana and arrange over the sponges. Cover with clingfilm and chill for 30 minutes.

3 To make the custard, put the egg yolks and sugar into a bowl and whisk together. Pour the milk into a pan and warm gently over a low heat. Remove from the heat and gradually stir into the egg mixture, then return the mixture to the pan and stir constantly over a low heat until thickened. Do not boil. Remove from the heat, pour into a bowl and stir in the vanilla. Cool for 1 hour. Spread the custard over the trifle sponge and fruit mixture, cover with clingfilm and chill for 2 hours.

4 To make the topping, whip the cream in a bowl and stir in sugar to taste. Spread over the trifle, then scatter over the chocolate. Cover with clingfilm and refrigerate for at least 2 hours before serving.

FESTIVE MINCE PIES

MAKES 12

200 g/7 oz plain flour, plus extra for
  dusting
100 g/3½ oz butter
25 g/1 oz icing sugar

1 egg yolk
2–3 tbsp milk
300 g/10½ oz mincemeat
1 egg, beaten, for sealing and glazing
icing sugar, for dusting

1 Preheat the oven to 180°C/350°F/Gas Mark 4. Sift the flour into a mixing bowl. Using your fingertips, rub in the butter until the mixture resembles breadcrumbs. Mix in the sugar and egg yolk.

2 Stir in enough milk to make a soft dough, turn out onto a lightly floured work surface and knead lightly until smooth.

3 Shape the dough into a ball and roll out to a thickness of 1 cm/½ inch. Use pastry cutters to cut out 12 rounds of 7 cm/2¾ inches diameter for the bases and 12 smaller star shapes for the tops. Dust 12 tartlet tins with flour and line with the dough rounds. Prick the bases with a fork, then half-fill each pie with mincemeat. Place the star shapes on top then brush all over with beaten egg. Bake in the preheated oven for 15 minutes. Remove from the oven and cool on a wire rack. Dust with icing sugar and serve.

SPICED CHRISTMAS PUNCH

SERVES 10
1 litre/1¾ pints of red wine
4 tbsp sugar
1 cinnamon stick
400 ml/14 fl oz boiling water
100 ml/3½ fl oz brandy
100 ml/3½ fl oz sherry

100 ml/3½ fl oz orange liqueur, such as
  Cointreau
2 seedless oranges, cut into wedges
2 dessert apples, cored and cut into
  wedges

GRANDMA'S TIPS

*You should use heatproof glasses
to serve this hot punch. If you
are concerned that your glasses
may be too fragile, place a metal
teaspoon in each glass as you
pour so that some of the heat is
absorbed by the metal.*

1 Put the wine, sugar and cinnamon into a large saucepan and stir together well. Warm over a low heat, stirring, until just starting to simmer, but do not let it boil. Remove from the heat and strain through a sieve. Discard the cinnamon stick.

2 Return the wine to the pan and stir in the water, brandy, sherry and orange liqueur. Add the orange and apple wedges and warm gently over a very low heat, but do not let it boil. Remove from the heat and pour into a large, heatproof punch bowl. Ladle into heatproof glasses and serve hot.

Those with a sweet tooth will fondly remember the delicious aromas of puddings and desserts that would emanate from Grandma's kitchen. Some are really quick and easy to assemble, whilst others take more time, making them best reserved for special occasions and family get-togethers. Profiteroles are always popular and together with banana splits and Black Forest gateau, will give even the most chocoholic cook enough recipes to indulge in. Pies, strudels and crumbles are included to add fruit to the menu – the fruit can

GRANDMA'S JUST DESSERTS

be changed according to taste and season, providing even more diversity. Along with the traditional favourites, such as baked apples, bread and butter pudding and good old rice pudding, you will find recipes for more exotic – but equally well-loved – desserts like Italian tiramisù and an American-style baked cheesecake. These are dishes that we've grown up with and adopted as our own, despite their far-flung origins. With such a wide selection you are certainly going to be spoilt for choice when it comes to choosing your Grandma's just dessert.

APPLE PIE

SERVES 6
for the pastry
350 g/12 oz plain flour
pinch of salt
85 g/3 oz butter or margarine, cut into
 small pieces
85 g/3 oz lard or white vegetable fat,
 cut into small pieces
about 6 tbsp cold water
beaten egg or milk, for glazing

for the filling
750 g–1 kg/1 lb 10 oz–2 lb 4 oz cooking
 apples, peeled, cored and sliced
125 g/4½ oz caster sugar, plus extra for
 sprinkling
½–1 tsp ground cinnamon, mixed spice
 or ground ginger
1–2 tbsp water (optional)

GRANDMA'S TIPS
*When preparing your apples
make sure you prepare them one
at a time, rather than peeling
them all and then slicing them.
Place the apple slices in a bowl
of water to which has been
added the juice of 1 lemon as
you go along – this will stop
them from discolouring.*

1 To make the pastry, sift the flour and salt into a mixing bowl. Add the butter and lard and rub in with your fingertips until the mixture resembles fine breadcrumbs. Add the water and gather the mixture together into a dough. Wrap the dough and chill in the refrigerator for 30 minutes.

2 Preheat the oven to 220°C/425°F/Gas Mark 7. Roll out almost two-thirds of the pastry thinly and use to line a deep 23-cm/9-inch pie plate or pie tin.

3 Mix the apples with the sugar and spice and pack into the pastry case; the filling can come up above the rim. Add the water if needed, particularly if the apples are not very juicy.

4 Roll out the remaining pastry to form a lid. Dampen the edges of the pie rim with water and position the lid, pressing the edges firmly together. Trim and crimp the edges.

5 Use the trimmings to cut out leaves or other shapes to decorate the top of the pie, dampen and attach. Glaze the top of the pie with beaten egg or milk, make 1–2 slits in the top and place the pie on a baking sheet.

6 Bake in the preheated oven for 20 minutes, then reduce the temperature to 180°C/ 350°F/Gas Mark 4 and bake for a further 30 minutes, or until the pastry is a light golden brown. Serve hot or cold, sprinkled with sugar.

LATTICED CHERRY PIE

SERVES 8
for the pastry
140 g/5 oz plain flour, plus extra for
 dusting
¼ tsp baking powder
½ tsp mixed spice
½ tsp salt
50 g/1¾ oz caster sugar
55 g/2 oz cold unsalted butter, diced,
 plus extra for greasing
1 beaten egg, plus extra for glazing
water, for sealing

for the filling
900 g/2 lb stoned fresh cherries, or
 canned cherries, drained
150 g/5½ oz caster sugar
½ tsp almond essence
2 tsp cherry brandy
¼ tsp mixed spice
2 tbsp cornflour
2 tbsp water
25 g/1 oz unsalted butter

freshly whipped cream or ice cream,
 to serve

GRANDMA'S TIPS

This pie can be made using other fruits, such as blackberries. To complement the blackberries, substitute 2 teaspoons of cassis liqueur for the cherry brandy.

1 To make the pastry, sift the flour with the baking powder into a large bowl. Stir in the mixed spice, salt and sugar. Using your fingertips, rub in the butter until the mixture resembles fine breadcrumbs, then make a well in the centre. Pour the beaten egg into the well. Mix with a wooden spoon, then shape the mixture into a dough. Cut the dough in half, and use your hands to roll each half into a ball. Wrap the dough and chill in the refrigerator for 30 minutes.

2 Preheat the oven to 220°C/425°F/Gas Mark 7. Grease a 23-cm/9-inch round pie dish with butter. Roll out the pastry into 2 rounds, each 30 cm/12 inches in diameter. Use one to line the pie dish. Trim the edges, leaving an overhang of 1 cm/½ inch.

3 To make the filling, put half of the cherries and the sugar in a large saucepan. Bring to a simmer over a low heat, stirring, for 5 minutes, or until the sugar has melted. Stir in the almond essence, brandy and mixed spice. In a separate bowl, mix the cornflour and water to form a paste. Remove the saucepan from the heat, stir in the cornflour paste, then return to the heat and stir constantly until the mixture boils and thickens. Leave to cool a little. Stir in the remaining cherries, pour into the pastry case, then dot with butter.

4 Cut the remaining pastry round into long strips 1 cm/½ inch wide. Lay the strips evenly on the top of the filling, crisscrossing to form a lattice. Trim off the ends and seal the edges with water. Use your fingers to crimp around the rim, then brush the top with beaten egg to glaze. Cover with kitchen foil, then bake for 30 minutes. Remove from the oven, discard the foil, then return the pie to the oven for a further 15 minutes, or until cooked and golden. Serve warm with freshly whipped cream or ice cream.

PEAR & PECAN STRUDEL

SERVES 4

2 ripe pears
55 g/2 oz butter
55 g/2 oz fresh white breadcrumbs
55 g/2 oz shelled pecan nuts, chopped
25 g/1 oz light muscovado sugar

finely grated rind of 1 orange
100 g/3½ oz filo pastry, thawed if frozen
6 tbsp orange blossom honey
2 tbsp orange juice
sifted icing sugar, for dusting
Greek-style yogurt, to serve (optional)

1 Preheat the oven to 200°C/400°F/Gas Mark 6. Peel, core and chop the pears. Melt 1 tablespoon of the butter in a frying pan and gently fry the breadcrumbs until golden. Transfer to a bowl and add the pears, nuts, muscovado sugar and orange rind. Put the remaining butter in a small saucepan and heat until melted.

2 Reserve 1 sheet of filo pastry, keeping it well wrapped, and brush the remaining filo sheets with a little melted butter. Spoon some of the nut filling onto the first filo sheet, leaving a 2.5-cm/1-inch margin around the edge. Build up the strudel by placing more buttered filo sheets on top of the first, spreading each one with nut filling as you build up the layers. Drizzle the honey and orange juice over the top.

3 Fold the short ends over the filling, then roll up, starting at a long side. Carefully lift onto a baking sheet, with the join facing up. Brush with any remaining melted butter and crumple the reserved sheet of filo pastry around the strudel. Bake for 25 minutes, or until golden and crisp. Dust with sifted icing sugar and serve warm with Greek-style yogurt, if using.

APPLE & BLACKBERRY
CRUMBLE

SERVES 4
900 g/2 lb cooking apples,
    peeled and sliced
300 g/10½ oz blackberries,
    fresh or frozen
55 g/2 oz light muscovado sugar
1 tsp ground cinnamon
single or double cream,
    to serve

crumble topping
85 g/3 oz self-raising flour
85 g/3 oz plain wholemeal flour
115 g/4 oz unsalted butter
55 g/2 oz demerara sugar

GRANDMA'S TIPS

*Make sure you use the freshest
fruit available as they will be
more flavoursome and sweet. A
handful of strawberries would be
a good addition as they enhance
the flavour and colour. In fact,
try substituting the apples and
blackberries for any of your
favourite fruits.*

1 Preheat the oven to 190°C/375°F/Gas Mark 5. Peel and core the apples and cut into chunks. Place in a bowl with the blackberries, muscovado sugar and cinnamon and mix together, then transfer to an ovenproof baking dish.

2 To make the crumble topping, sift the self-raising flour into a bowl and stir in the wholemeal flour. Add the unsalted butter and rub in with your fingers until the mixture resembles fine breadcrumbs. Stir in the demerara sugar.

3 Spread the crumble over the apples and bake in the preheated oven for 40–45 minutes, or until the apples are soft and the crumble is golden brown and crisp. Serve hot with cream.

LEMON MERINGUE PIE

SERVES 4
for the pastry
150 g/5½ oz plain flour, plus extra for
   dusting
85 g/3 oz butter, cut into small pieces,
   plus extra for greasing
35 g/1¼ oz icing sugar, sifted
finely grated rind of ½ lemon
½ egg yolk, beaten
1½ tbsp milk

for the filling
3 tbsp cornflour
300 ml/10 fl oz water
juice and grated rind of 2 lemons
175 g/6 oz caster sugar
2 eggs, separated

GRANDMA'S TIPS

This dessert is usually served cold, but why not try it hot? It may sound rather decadent but hot lemon meringue pie with cold ice cream is to die for. Lime or orange juice and rind may be substituted for the lemon juice and rind for a change.

1 To make the pastry, sift the flour into a bowl. Rub in the butter with your fingertips until the mixture resembles fine breadcrumbs. Mix in the remaining ingredients. Knead briefly on a lightly floured work surface. Rest for 30 minutes.

2 Preheat the oven to 180°C/350°F/Gas Mark 4. Grease a 20-cm/8-inch pie dish with butter. Roll out the pastry to a thickness of 5 mm/¼ inch; use it to line the base and sides of the dish. Prick all over with a fork, line with baking paper and fill with baking beans. Bake for 15 minutes. Remove the pastry case from the oven and take out the paper and beans. Reduce the temperature to 150°C/300°F/Gas Mark 2.

3 To make the filling, mix the cornflour with a little of the water. Put the remaining water in a saucepan. Stir in the lemon juice and rind and cornflour paste. Bring to the boil, stirring.

4 Cook for 2 minutes. Cool a little. Stir in 5 tablespoons of the sugar and the egg yolks and pour into the pastry case.

5 Whisk the egg whites in a clean, grease-free bowl until stiff. Gradually whisk in the remaining sugar and spread over the pie. Bake for a further 40 minutes. Remove from oven, cool and serve.

RICH VANILLA ICE CREAM

SERVES 4–6

300 ml/10 fl oz single cream and
   300 ml/10 fl oz double cream
   or 600 ml/1 pint whipping cream

1 vanilla pod
4 large egg yolks
100 g/3½ oz caster sugar

1 Pour the single and double cream or whipping cream into a large heavy-based saucepan. Split open the vanilla pod and scrape out the seeds into the cream, then add the whole vanilla pod, too. Bring almost to the boil, then remove from the heat and infuse for 30 minutes.

2 Put the egg yolks and sugar in a large bowl and whisk together until pale and the mixture leaves a trail when the whisk is lifted. Remove the vanilla pod from the cream, then slowly add the cream to the egg mixture, stirring all the time with a wooden spoon. Strain the mixture into the rinsed-out pan or a double boiler and cook over a low heat for 10–15 minutes, stirring all the time, until the mixture thickens enough to coat the back of the spoon. Do not let the mixture boil or it will curdle. Remove from the heat and cool for at least 1 hour, stirring from time to time to prevent a skin forming.

3 Churn the custard in an ice cream maker, following the manufacturer's instructions. Serve immediately if wished, or transfer to a freezerproof container, cover with a lid and store in the freezer.

BREAD & BUTTER PUDDING

SERVES 4–6
85 g/3 oz butter, softened
6 slices of thick white bread
55 g/2 oz mixed fruit (sultanas, currants
 and raisins)
25 g/1 oz candied peel
3 large eggs

300 ml/10 fl oz milk
150 ml/5 fl oz double cream
55 g/2 oz caster sugar
whole nutmeg, for grating
1 tbsp demerara sugar
cream, to serve

GRANDMA'S TIPS

*Try using brioche or a lightly
fruited loaf instead of the white
bread. Any mixture of dried
fruits can be used – why not
experiment with your favourites?
Dried apricots, cherries and
cranberries are all nice.*

1 Preheat the oven to 180°C/350°F/Gas Mark 4.

2 Use a little of the butter to grease a 20 x 25-cm/8 x 10-inch baking dish and butter the slices of bread. Cut the bread into quarters and arrange half overlapping in the dish.

3 Scatter half the fruit and peel over the bread, cover with the remaining bread slices and add the remaining fruit and peel.

4 In a mixing jug, whisk the eggs well and mix in the milk, cream and sugar. Pour this over the pudding and leave to stand for 15 minutes to allow the bread to soak up some of the egg mixture. Tuck in most of the fruit as you don't want it to burn in the oven. Grate the nutmeg over the top of the pudding, according to taste, and sprinkle over the demerara sugar.

5 Place the pudding on a baking tray and bake at the top of the oven for 30–40 minutes until just set and golden brown.

6 Remove from the oven and serve warm with a little pouring cream.

STICKY TOFFEE PUDDING

SERVES 4
for the pudding
75 g/2¾ oz sultanas
150 g/5½ oz stoned dates, chopped
1 tsp bicarbonate of soda
2 tbsp butter, plus extra for greasing
200 g/7 oz brown sugar
2 eggs
200 g/7 oz self-raising flour, sifted

for the sticky toffee sauce
2 tbsp butter
175 ml/6 fl oz double cream
200 g/7 oz brown sugar

zested orange rind, to decorate
freshly whipped cream, to serve

GRANDMA'S TIPS
You can make this wicked pudding in individual pudding basins so that everyone has their own portion. Cook for 20–25 minutes and then turn out onto serving plates. This dessert is delicious served with whipped cream, ice cream or clotted cream.

1 To make the pudding, put the sultanas, dates and bicarbonate of soda into a heatproof bowl. Cover with boiling water and leave to soak.

2 Preheat the oven to 180°C/350°F/Gas Mark 4. Grease a round cake tin, 20 cm/8 inches in diameter, with butter.

3 Put the remaining butter in a separate bowl, add the sugar and mix well. Beat in the eggs then fold in the flour. Drain the soaked fruits, add to the bowl and mix. Spoon the mixture evenly into the prepared cake tin. Transfer to the preheated oven and bake for 35–40 minutes. The pudding is cooked when a skewer inserted into the centre comes out clean.

4 About 5 minutes before the end of the cooking time, make the sauce. Melt the butter in a saucepan over a medium heat. Stir in the cream and sugar and bring to the boil, stirring constantly. Lower the heat and simmer for 5 minutes.

5 Turn out the pudding onto a serving plate and pour over the sauce. Decorate with zested orange rind and serve with whipped cream.

NEW YORK CHEESECAKE WITH BLUEBERRY COMPOTE

SERVES 8–10
sunflower oil, for brushing
85 g/3 oz unsalted butter
200 g/7 oz digestive biscuits, crushed
450 g/1 lb full-fat cream cheese
100 g/3½ oz caster sugar
2 large eggs
1 large egg yolk
100 ml/3½ fl oz soured cream
1½ tsp vanilla essence

for the topping
400 ml/14 fl oz soured cream
55 g/2 oz caster sugar

for the blueberry compote
55 g/2 oz caster sugar
4 tbsp water
250 g/9 oz fresh blueberries
1 tsp arrowroot

1 Preheat the oven to 150°C/300°F/Gas Mark 2. Brush a 20-cm/8-inch springform cake pan with oil. Melt the butter in a saucepan over a low heat. Stir in the digestive biscuits and press evenly into the base of the pan. Bake for 10 minutes, or until lightly browned, then remove and set aside to cool.

2 Place the cream cheese into a large bowl and beat until smooth. Add the sugar and beat for 1 minute. Add the eggs and egg yolk and beat until well combined. Add the soured cream and vanilla essence and stir until smooth. Pour the mixture into the pan and spread evenly.

3 Bake in the oven for 35–45 minutes or until the edges are firm but the centre is still slightly soft.

4 Remove from the oven and place on a wire rack (still in the pan). Increase the oven temperature to 200°C/400°F/Gas Mark 6.

5 To make the topping, mix together the soured cream and caster sugar, and spread over the top of the cheesecake. Place in the oven and bake for 5–7 minutes until the topping has become very liquid. Turn the oven off but leave the cheesecake inside for 1 hour. Remove from the oven and cool in the pan on a wire rack. Cover and refrigerate overnight.

6 To make the compote, combine the sugar and half the water in a small saucepan and stir over a low heat until the sugar has dissolved. Increase the heat, add the blueberries, then cover and cook for 2–3 minutes or until the blueberries begin to soften. Remove from the heat. Stir together the arrowroot and remaining water in a cup to dissolve the arrowroot. Add to the fruit, return to a low heat, and stir until the juice thickens and turns translucent. Leave to cool completely.

7 Remove the cheesecake from the pan 30 minutes before serving. Spoon the fruit on top and chill until ready to serve.

BLACK FOREST GATEAU

SERVES 8

3 tbsp unsalted butter, melted, plus extra
   for greasing
900 g/2 lb fresh cherries, stoned and
   halved
250 g/9 oz caster sugar
100 ml/3½ fl oz cherry brandy
100 g/3½ oz plain flour

50 g/1¾ oz cocoa powder
½ tsp baking powder
4 eggs
1 litre/1¾ pints double cream

to decorate
grated dark chocolate
whole fresh cherries

GRANDMA'S TIPS

*It is possible to make this
extravagant gateau using canned
cherries – drain the fruit from
the juice and use the liquid to
soak the cake before assembling.
Kirsch or brandy can be used
instead of the cherry brandy.*

1 Preheat the oven to 180°C/350°F/Gas Mark 4. Grease and line a 23-cm/9-inch springform cake pan. Place the cherries in a saucepan, add 3 tablespoons of the sugar and the cherry brandy and bring to a simmer over medium heat. Simmer for 5 minutes. Drain, reserving the syrup. In a large bowl, sift together the flour, cocoa, and baking powder.

2 Place the eggs in a heatproof bowl and beat in 160 g/5¾ oz of the sugar. Place the bowl over a saucepan of simmering water and beat for 6 minutes, or until thickened. Remove from the heat, then gradually fold in the flour mixture and melted butter. Spoon into the cake pan and bake for 40 minutes. Remove from the oven and leave to cool in the pan.

3 Turn out the cake and cut in half horizontally. Mix the double cream and the remaining sugar together and whip lightly until soft peaks form. Spread the reserved syrup over the cut sides of the cake, then spread a layer of whipped cream on the bottom half of the cake, followed by the cherries, and then place the other half on top. Cover the top of the cake with whipped cream, sprinkle over the grated chocolate and decorate with whole fresh cherries.

PROFITEROLES

SERVES 4
for the choux pastry
5 tbsp butter, plus extra for greasing
200 ml/7 fl oz cold water
100 g/3½ oz plain flour
3 eggs, beaten

for the cream filling
300 ml/10 fl oz double cream
3 tbsp caster sugar
1 tsp vanilla essence

for the chocolate & brandy sauce
125 g/4½ oz plain dark chocolate,
   broken into pieces
2½ tbsp butter
6 tbsp water
2 tbsp brandy

GRANDMA'S TIPS
*The choux puffs can be made
two to three days ahead and kept
in an airtight container until
needed. The empty puffs can also
be filled with savoury mixtures,
like prawns and mayonnaise, to
serve with drinks.*

1 Preheat the oven to 200°C/400°F/Gas Mark 6.

2 Grease a large baking sheet with butter. To make the pastry, place the water and butter in a saucepan and bring to the boil. Meanwhile, sift the flour into a bowl. Remove the saucepan from the heat and beat in the flour until smooth. Cool for 5 minutes. Beat in enough of the eggs to give the mixture a soft, dropping consistency. Transfer to a piping bag fitted with a 1-cm/½-inch plain nozzle. Pipe small balls onto the baking sheet. Bake for 25 minutes. Remove from the oven. Pierce each ball with a skewer to let steam escape.

3 To make the filling, whip together the cream, sugar and vanilla essence. Cut the pastry balls almost in half, then fill with the cream filling.

4 To make the sauce, gently melt the chocolate and butter with the water in a small saucepan, stirring, until smooth. Stir in the brandy. Pile the profiteroles into individual serving dishes or into a pyramid on a raised cake stand. Pour over the sauce and serve.

SPOTTED DICK &
CUSTARD

SERVES 6
225 g/8 oz self-raising flour,
  plus extra for dusting
115 g/4 oz suet
55 g/2 oz caster sugar
140 g/5 oz currants or raisins
grated rind of 1 lemon
150–175 ml/5–6 fl oz milk
2 tsp melted butter, for greasing

custard
425 ml/15 fl oz single cream
5 egg yolks
3 tbsp caster sugar
½ tsp vanilla extract
1 tsp cornflour (optional)

1 Mix together the flour, suet, sugar, currants and lemon rind in a mixing bowl.

2 Pour in the milk and stir together to give a fairly soft dough.

3 Turn out onto a floured surface and roll into a cylinder. Wrap in greaseproof paper that has been well-buttered and seal the ends, allowing room for the pudding to rise. Overwrap with foil and place in a steamer over a saucepan of boiling water.

4 Steam for about 1–1½ hours, checking the water level in the saucepan from time to time.

5 To make the custard, heat the cream in a small saucepan just to boiling point. Cream the egg yolks, sugar and vanilla extract together in a measuring jug. You can add the cornflour to this cold egg yolk mixture to ensure the sauce does not separate. Pour the hot cream into the jug, stirring all the time. Return the mixture to the saucepan.

6 Heat the custard very gently, stirring constantly, until the sauce has just thickened, then remove from the heat. Alternatively, you can cook the custard in a bowl over a saucepan of simmering water to prevent overcooking.

7 Remove the pudding from the steamer and unwrap. Place on a hot plate and cut into thick slices. Serve with lots of custard.

TRADITIONAL TIRAMISU

SERVES 6

20–24 sponge fingers, about 150 g/5½ oz
2 tbsp cold black coffee
2 tbsp coffee essence
2 tbsp almond liqueur
4 egg yolks
85 g/3 oz caster sugar
a few drops of vanilla essence

grated rind of ½ lemon
350 g/12 oz mascarpone cheese
2 tsp lemon juice
250 ml/9 fl oz double cream
1 tbsp milk
25 g/1 oz lightly toasted flaked almonds
2 tbsp cocoa powder
1 tbsp icing sugar

GRANDMA'S TIPS

This wonderful Italian dessert – a literal translation is 'pick me up' – is very rich and should be served in small portions. A glass of Amaretto is the perfect accompaniment. This dessert looks equally as divine when served in individual ramekins – divide the ingredients accordingly for mouth-watering results.

1 Arrange almost half of the sponge fingers in the base of a serving dish. Place the black coffee, coffee essence and almond liqueur in a bowl and mix. Sprinkle just over half of the mixture over the sponge fingers.

2 Place the egg yolks in a heatproof bowl with the sugar, vanilla essence and lemon rind. Stand the bowl over a saucepan of gently simmering water and whisk until very thick and creamy and the whisk leaves a heavy trail when lifted from the bowl.

3 Place the mascarpone cheese in a separate bowl with the lemon juice and beat until smooth. Stir into the egg mixture and, when evenly blended, pour half of the mixture over the sponge fingers and spread out evenly.

4 Add another layer of sponge fingers, sprinkle with the remaining coffee mixture, then cover with the rest of the cheese and egg mixture. Leave to chill in the refrigerator for at least 2 hours, preferably overnight.

5 Whip the cream and milk together until fairly stiff and spread or pipe over the dessert. Sprinkle with the flaked almonds, then sift an even layer of cocoa powder over the top to cover completely. Finally, sift a layer of icing sugar over the cocoa powder and serve.

BAKED RICE PUDDING

SERVES 4–6
1 tbsp melted unsalted butter
115 g/4 oz pudding rice
55 g/2 oz caster sugar
850 ml/1½ pints full-cream milk
½ tsp vanilla essence

40 g/1½ oz unsalted butter, chilled and
  cut into pieces
whole nutmeg, for grating
cream, jam, fresh fruit purée, stewed
  fruit, honey or ice cream, to serve

GRANDMA'S TIPS

In place of nutmeg, you can try grated lemon rind or another spice such as cinnamon to flavour the rice pudding. A handful of raisins or other dried fruit can be added before cooking. If you wish, the rice pudding may be cooked in individual ramekins – just reduce the cooking time to 1–1½ hours.

1 Preheat the oven to 150ºC/300ºF/Gas Mark 2. Grease a 1.2-litre/2-pint baking dish (a gratin dish is good) with the melted butter, place the rice in the dish and sprinkle with the sugar.

2 Heat the milk in a saucepan until almost boiling, then pour over the rice. Add the vanilla essence and stir well to dissolve the sugar.

3 Cut the butter into small pieces and scatter over the surface of the pudding.

4 Grate the whole nutmeg over the top, using as much as you like to give a good covering.

5 Place the dish on a baking tray and bake in the centre of the oven for 1½–2 hours until the pudding is well browned on the top. You can stir it after the first half hour to disperse the rice.

6 Serve hot topped with cream, jam, fresh fruit purée, stewed fruit, honey or ice cream.

BAKED APPLES

SERVES 4
25 g/1 oz blanched almonds
55 g/2 oz dried apricots
1 piece stem ginger, drained
1 tbsp clear honey

1 tbsp syrup from the stem ginger jar
4 tbsp rolled oats
4 large cooking apples

1 Preheat the oven to 180°C/350°F/Gas Mark 4. Using a sharp knife, chop the almonds very finely. Chop the apricots and stem ginger very finely. Reserve.

2 Place the honey and syrup in a saucepan and heat until the honey has melted. Stir in the oats and cook gently over a low heat for 2 minutes. Remove the saucepan from the heat and stir in the almonds, apricots and stem ginger.

3 Core the apples, widen the tops slightly and score around the circumference of each to prevent the skins bursting during cooking. Place them in an ovenproof dish and fill the cavities with the stuffing. Pour just enough water into the dish to come about one-third of the way up the apples. Bake in the preheated oven for 40 minutes, or until tender. Serve immediately.

BLUEBERRY PANCAKES

MAKES 10–12
140 g/5 oz plain flour
2 tbsp caster sugar
2 tbsp baking powder
½ tsp salt
225 ml/8 fl oz buttermilk
3 tbsp butter, melted

1 large egg
140 g/5 oz fresh blueberries, plus
  extra to serve
sunflower oil, for oiling
butter and warmed maple syrup,
  to serve

GRANDMA'S TIPS

*These small pancakes are ideal
to serve for breakfast with crispy
bacon or scrambled eggs and any
other accompaniment of your
choice.*

1 Preheat the oven to 140°C/275°F/Gas Mark 1. Sieve the flour, sugar, baking powder and salt together into a large bowl and make a well in the centre.

2 Beat the buttermilk, butter and egg together in a separate small bowl, then pour the mixture into the well in the dry ingredients. Beat the dry ingredients into the liquid, gradually drawing them in from the side, until a smooth batter is formed. Gently stir in the blueberries.

3 Heat a large frying pan over a medium-high heat until a splash of water dances on the surface. Using a pastry brush or crumpled piece of kitchen paper, oil the base of the frying pan.

4 Drop about 4 tablespoons of batter separately into the frying pan and spread each out into a 10-cm/4-inch round. Continue adding as many pancakes as will fit in your frying pan. Cook until small bubbles appear on the surface, then flip over with a spatula or palette knife and cook the pancakes on the other side for a further 1–2 minutes until golden brown.

5 Transfer the pancakes to a warmed plate and keep warm in the preheated oven while you cook the remaining batter, lightly oiling the frying pan as before. Make a stack of the pancakes with baking paper in between each pancake.

6 Serve with a knob of butter on top of each pancake and warm maple syrup for pouring over.

BANANA SPLITS

SERVES 4
4 bananas
6 tbsp chopped mixed nuts, to serve

for the vanilla ice cream
300 ml/10 fl oz milk
1 tsp vanilla essence
3 egg yolks
100 g/3½ oz caster sugar
300 ml/10 fl oz double cream, whipped

for the chocolate rum sauce
125 g/4½ oz plain chocolate, broken into
  small pieces
2½ tbsp butter
6 tbsp water
1 tbsp rum

GRANDMA'S TIPS
*For a quick and easy pudding,
use shop-bought ice cream. If
you're serving the banana splits
to children, omit the rum from
the chocolate sauce.*

1 To make the ice cream, heat the milk and vanilla essence in a saucepan until almost boiling. In a bowl, beat together the egg yolks and sugar. Remove the milk from the heat and stir a little into the egg mixture. Transfer the mixture to the pan. Stir over a low heat until thick. Do not boil. Remove from the heat. Cool for 30 minutes, fold in the cream, cover with clingfilm and chill for 1 hour. Transfer into an ice-cream maker and process for 15 minutes. Alternatively, transfer into a freezerproof container and freeze for 1 hour, then place in a bowl and beat to break up the ice crystals. Put back in the container and freeze for 30 minutes. Repeat twice more, freezing for 30 minutes and whisking each time.

2 To make the sauce, melt the chocolate and butter with the water in a saucepan, stirring. Remove from the heat and stir in the rum. Peel the bananas, slice lengthways and arrange on 4 serving dishes. Top with ice cream and nuts and serve with the sauce.

Remember the smells of home-baked cakes, biscuits and scones when
you were young? It was on those days that you learned to rub fat
into flour with your fingertips to make pastry and to beat sugar
and butter together to make cakes. It was fun to sprinkle flour over
the kitchen table, roll out biscuit dough and cut it into different
shapes – Grandma didn't seem to mind the mess. The best bit was
eating the misshapen bits when they were still hot from the oven.
This chapter provides recipes for all kinds of delicious goodies – from

GRANDMA'S BAKING DAY

a classic Victoria sponge cake to indulgent chocolate chip cookies.
Perhaps it will even encourage you to bake with your own children
or grandchildren – they will particularly enjoy helping to make the
easy nutty flapjacks or assembling the lemon butterfly cakes. All of
the recipes in this section are perfect for filling those little gaps in
the day, be it mid-morning or tea-time – but make sure you put
the rest away in an airtight tin so that there is always something
delicious to hand when friends or family come by.

VICTORIA SPONGE CAKE

SERVES 8–10

175 g/6 oz butter, at room temperature,
plus extra for greasing
175 g/6 oz caster sugar
3 eggs, beaten

175 g/6 oz self-raising flour
pinch of salt
3 tbsp raspberry jam
1 tbsp caster or icing sugar

GRANDMA'S TIPS

These cakes can also be flavoured with grated lemon rind and sandwiched together with lemon curd for a summery feel. For a simple butter cream filling, beat together equal quantities of butter and icing sugar until light and fluffy.

1 Preheat the oven to 180°C/350°F/Gas Mark 4.

2 Grease two 20-cm/8-inch sponge tins and line with greaseproof paper or baking paper.

3 Cream the butter and sugar together in a mixing bowl using a wooden spoon or a hand-held mixer until the mixture is pale in colour and light and fluffy.

4 Add the egg a little at a time, beating well after each addition.

5 Sift the flour and salt and carefully add to the mixture, folding it in with a metal spoon or a spatula.

6 Divide the mixture between the tins and smooth over with the spatula.

7 Place them on the same shelf in the centre of the oven and bake for 25–30 minutes until well risen, golden brown and beginning to shrink from the sides of the tin.

8 Remove from the oven and allow to stand for 1 minute.

9 Loosen the cakes from around the edge of the tins using a palette knife. Turn the cakes out onto a clean tea towel, remove the paper and invert them onto a wire rack (this prevents the wire rack from marking the top of the cakes).

10 When completely cool, sandwich together with the jam and sprinkle with the sugar. The cake is delicious when freshly baked, but any remaining cake can be stored in an airtight tin for up to 1 week.

LEMON DRIZZLE CAKE

SERVES 8
butter, for greasing
200 g/7 oz plain flour
2 tsp baking powder
200 g/7 oz caster sugar
4 eggs
150 ml/5 fl oz soured cream
grated rind of 1 large lemon
4 tbsp lemon juice
150 ml/5 fl oz sunflower oil

for the syrup
4 tbsp icing sugar
3 tbsp lemon juice

GRANDMA'S TIPS

Give the cake a summery flavour by serving with tangy crème fraîche and some summer berries such as blueberries, raspberries and blackcurrants.

1 Preheat the oven to 180°C/350°F/Gas Mark 4. Lightly grease a 20-cm/8-inch loose-bottom round cake tin and line the base with baking paper.

2 Sieve the flour and baking powder into a mixing bowl and stir in the caster sugar.

3 In a separate bowl, whisk the eggs, soured cream, lemon rind, lemon juice and oil together.

4 Pour the egg mixture into the dry ingredients and mix well until evenly combined.

5 Pour the mixture into the prepared tin and bake in the preheated oven for 45–60 minutes until risen and golden brown.

6 Meanwhile, to make the syrup, mix together the icing sugar and lemon juice in a small saucepan. Stir over a low heat until just beginning to bubble and turn syrupy.

7 As soon as the cake comes out of the oven, prick the surface with a fine skewer, then brush the syrup over the top. Leave the cake to cool completely in the tin before turning out and serving.

RICH FRUIT CAKE

SERVES 12
butter, for greasing
175 g/6 oz stoned unsweetened dates
125 g/4½ oz ready-to-eat dried prunes
200 ml/7 fl oz unsweetened orange juice
2 tbsp black treacle
1 tsp finely grated lemon rind
1 tsp finely grated orange rind
225 g/8 oz wholemeal self-raising flour
1 tsp mixed spice
125 g/4½ oz seedless raisins
125 g/4½ oz sultanas
125 g/4½ oz currants
125 g/4½ oz dried cranberries
3 large eggs, separated

to decorate
1 tbsp apricot jam, warmed
icing sugar, for dusting
175 g/6 oz sugar paste
strips of orange rind
strips of lemon rind

1 Grease and line a deep 20-cm/8-inch round cake tin. Chop the dates and prunes and place in a large, heavy-based saucepan. Pour over the orange juice and simmer for 10 minutes. Remove the saucepan from the heat and beat the fruit mixture until puréed. Add the treacle and citrus rinds and leave to cool.

2 Preheat the oven to 160°C/325°F/Gas Mark 3. Sift the flour and mixed spice into a bowl, adding any bran that remains in the sieve. Add the raisins, sultanas, currants and dried cranberries. When the date and prune mixture is cool, whisk in the egg yolks. Whisk the egg whites in a clean bowl until stiff. Spoon the fruit mixture into the dry ingredients and mix together. Gently fold in the egg whites. Transfer to the prepared tin and bake in the preheated oven for 1½ hours. Leave to cool in the tin.

3 Remove the cake from the tin and brush the top with jam. Dust the work surface with icing sugar and roll out the sugar paste thinly. Lay the sugar paste over the top of the cake and trim the edges. Decorate with orange and lemon rind.

CLASSIC CARROT CAKE

SERVES 12
butter, for greasing
125 g/4½ oz self-raising flour
pinch of salt
1 tsp ground cinnamon
125 g/4½ oz soft brown sugar
2 eggs
100 ml/3½ fl oz sunflower oil
125 g/4½ oz carrot, peeled and
  finely grated
25 g/1 oz desiccated coconut
25 g/1 oz walnuts, chopped
walnut pieces, to decorate

icing
50 g/1¾ oz butter, softened
50 g/1¾ oz soft cheese
225 g/8 oz icing sugar, sifted
1 tsp lemon juice

GRANDMA'S TIPS

This cake freezes well (without the icing) and can be kept for up to three months. It's perfect for a teatime treat as well as a quick dessert served with some ice cream.

1 Preheat the oven to 180°C/350°F/Gas Mark 4. Lightly grease a 20-cm/8-inch square cake tin and line the base with baking paper.

2 Sift the flour, salt and ground cinnamon into a large bowl and stir in the brown sugar. Add the eggs and oil to the dry ingredients and mix well.

3 Stir in the grated carrot, desiccated coconut and chopped walnuts.

4 Pour the mixture into the prepared tin and bake in the preheated oven for 20–25 minutes, or until just firm to the touch. Leave to cool in the tin.

5 Meanwhile, make the icing. In a bowl, beat together the butter, soft cheese, icing sugar and lemon juice until the mixture is fluffy and creamy.

6 Turn the cake out of the tin and cut into 12 bars or slices. Spread with the icing and then decorate with walnut pieces.

APPLE STREUSEL CAKE

SERVES 8
115 g/4 oz butter, plus extra for greasing
450 g/1 lb cooking apples
175 g/6 oz self-raising flour
1 tsp ground cinnamon
pinch of salt
115 g/4 oz caster sugar
2 eggs
1–2 tbsp milk
icing sugar, for dusting

streusel topping
115 g/4 oz self-raising flour
85 g/3 oz butter
85 g/3 oz caster sugar

GRANDMA'S TIPS

This moist Streusel Cake not only makes a great dessert. It's good for breakfast or coffee breaks as well. Try it warm from the oven topped with some cream or a scoop of vanilla ice cream.

1 Preheat the oven to 180°C/350°F/Gas Mark 4, then grease a 23-cm/9-inch springform cake tin. To make the streusel topping, sift the flour into a bowl and rub in the butter until the mixture resembles coarse crumbs. Stir in the sugar and reserve.

2 Peel, core and thinly slice the apples. To make the cake, sift the flour into a bowl with the cinnamon and salt. Place the butter and sugar in a separate bowl and beat together until light and fluffy. Gradually beat in the eggs, adding a little of the flour mixture with the last addition of egg. Gently fold in half the remaining flour mixture, then fold in the rest with the milk.

3 Spoon the mixture into the prepared tin and smooth the top. Cover with the sliced apples and sprinkle the streusel topping evenly over the top. Bake in the preheated oven for 1 hour, or until browned and firm to the touch. Leave to cool in the tin before opening the sides. Dust the cake with icing sugar before serving.

COFFEE &
WALNUT CAKE

SERVES 8

icing
6 tbsp cocoa powder
2 tbsp cornflour
6 tbsp caster sugar
125 ml/4 fl oz strong black coffee,
  cooled
250 ml/9 fl oz milk
walnut halves, to decorate

sponge
85 g/3 oz butter, softened,
  plus extra for greasing
275 g/9½ oz plain flour
1 tbsp baking powder
85 g/3 oz caster sugar
2 eggs
150 ml/5 fl oz milk
3 tbsp hot strong black coffee
60 g/2¼ oz shelled walnuts, chopped
50 g/1¾ oz sultanas

1 To make the icing, put all the ingredients into a food processor and process until creamy. Transfer to a saucepan and heat, stirring, over a medium heat until bubbling. Cook for 1 minute, then pour into a heatproof bowl. Leave to cool, then cover with clingfilm and refrigerate for at least 2 hours.

2 Preheat the oven to 190°C/375°F/Gas Mark 5. Grease a 23-cm/9-inch loose-bottomed cake tin with butter and line with baking paper. To make the sponge, sift the flour and baking powder into a bowl, then stir in the sugar. In a separate bowl, beat together the butter, eggs, milk and coffee, then mix into the flour mixture.

3 Stir in the chopped walnuts and the sultanas. Spoon the mixture into the prepared cake tin and level the surface. Transfer to the preheated oven and bake for 1 hour. Remove from the oven and leave to cool. When cool enough to handle, turn out on to a wire rack and leave to cool completely. Spread the icing over the top of the cooled cake, decorate with the walnut halves and serve.

GINGERBREAD

MAKES 12–16
450 g/1 lb plain flour
3 tsp baking powder
1 tsp bicarbonate of soda
3 tsp ground ginger
175 g/6 oz unsalted butter
175 g/6 oz soft brown sugar

175 g/6 oz black treacle
175 g/6 oz golden syrup
1 egg, beaten
300 ml/10 fl oz milk
cream or warmed golden syrup,
   to serve

GRANDMA'S TIPS

A very moist gingerbread is a delight. It can be made even better by mixing in 55 g/2 oz chopped preserved stem ginger just before putting the mixture into the tin.

1 Line a 23-cm/9-inch square cake tin, 5 cm/2 inches deep, with greaseproof or baking paper.

2 Preheat the oven to 160°C/325°F/Gas Mark 3.

3 Sift the flour, baking powder, bicarbonate of soda and ground ginger into a large mixing bowl.

4 Place the butter, sugar, treacle and syrup in a medium saucepan and heat over a low heat until the butter has melted and the sugar dissolved. Allow to cool a little.

5 Mix the beaten egg with the milk and add to the cooled syrup mixture.

6 Add all the liquid ingredients to the flour mixture and beat well using a wooden spoon until the mixture is smooth and glossy.

7 Pour the mixture into the prepared tin and bake in the centre of the oven for 1½ hours until well risen and just firm to the touch. This gives a lovely sticky gingerbread, but if you like a firmer cake cook for a further 15 minutes.

8 Remove from the oven and allow the cake to cool in the tin. When cool, remove the cake from the tin with the lining paper. Over wrap with foil and place in an airtight tin for up to 1 week to allow the flavours to mature.

9 Cut into wedges and serve cold with tea or coffee or warm with cream and golden syrup.

MARBLED CHOCOLATE &
ORANGE TEABREAD

SERVES 12
150 g/5½ oz butter, softened,
  plus extra for greasing
75 g/2¾ oz plain chocolate,
  broken into pieces
250 g/9 oz caster sugar

5 large eggs, beaten
150 g/5½ oz plain flour
2 tsp baking powder
pinch of salt
grated rind of 2 oranges

GRANDMA'S TIPS

*If you prefer bananas to
oranges, or just fancy a change,
substitute the orange rinds for
some banana pieces to add a
completely different flavour.*

1 Preheat the oven to 180°C/350°F/Gas Mark 4. Grease and line the base and ends of two 450-g/1-lb loaf tins. Place the chocolate in a heatproof bowl set over a saucepan of simmering water, making sure that the base of the bowl does not touch the water. Remove from the heat once the chocolate has melted.

2 Place the butter and sugar in a separate bowl and beat until light and fluffy. Gradually beat in the eggs. Sift the flour, baking powder and salt into the mixture and fold in.

3 Transfer one-third of the mixture to the melted chocolate and stir together. Stir the orange rind into the remaining mixture and place one-quarter of the mixture in each cake tin, spread in an even layer.

4 Drop spoonfuls of the chocolate mixture on top, dividing it between the 2 tins, but do not smooth it out. Divide the remaining orange mixture between the 2 tins, then, using a knife, gently swirl the top 2 layers together to give a marbled effect. Bake in the preheated oven for 35–40 minutes, or until a skewer inserted into the centre comes out clean.

5 Leave to cool in the tins for 10 minutes, then turn out, peel off the lining paper and transfer to a wire rack to cool completely.

BANANA COCONUT
LOAF CAKE

MAKES 1 LOAF

90 ml/3 fl oz sunflower oil,
  plus extra for greasing
250 g/9 oz plain flour
1 ½ tsp baking powder
200 g/7 oz caster sugar

55 g/2 oz desiccated coconut
2 eggs
2 ripe bananas, mashed
125 ml/4 fl oz soured cream
1 tsp vanilla extract
long shred coconut, toasted, to decorate

1 Preheat the oven to 180°C/350°F/Gas Mark 4. Grease and line a 1-litre/1¾ pint loaf tin. Sift together the flour and baking powder in a large bowl and stir in the sugar and coconut.

2 Beat together the eggs, oil, bananas, cream and vanilla extract in a large bowl. Stir into the dry ingredients, mixing until evenly combined. Spoon into the prepared tin, levelling with a palette knife.

3 Bake in the preheated oven for about 1 hour or until risen, firm and golden brown. Cool in the tin for 15 minutes, then turn out onto a wire rack to cool completely. Decorate with shreds of coconut and serve.

STRAWBERRY ROULADE

SERVES 8
3 large eggs
125 g/4½ oz caster sugar
125 g/4½ oz plain flour
1 tbsp hot water

filling
200 ml/7 fl oz low-fat fromage frais
1 tsp almond essence
225 g/8 oz small strawberries
15 g/½ oz flaked almonds, toasted
icing sugar, for dusting

GRANDMA'S TIPS

Making a roulade looks quite difficult, but it really is quite simple when you use baking paper. Try varying the filling by using raspberries instead of the strawberries or whipped cream instead of the mascarpone. For a simple roulade, fill with jam – this makes a good base for a trifle.

1 Preheat the oven to 220°C/425°F/Gas Mark 7. Line a 35 x 25-cm/14 x 10-inch Swiss roll tin with baking paper. Place the eggs in a large, heatproof bowl with the caster sugar, place over a saucepan of hot water and, using an electric beater, beat until pale and thick.

2 Remove the bowl from the saucepan. Sift in the flour and fold into the eggs with the hot water. Pour the mixture into the prepared tin and bake in the preheated oven for 8–10 minutes, or until golden and set.

3 Transfer the sponge to a sheet of baking paper. Peel off the lining paper and roll up the sponge tightly along with the baking paper. Wrap in a tea towel and cool until completely cooled.

4 Mix the fromage frais and almond essence together in a bowl. Leave the mixture to chill in the refrigerator until required. Wash, hull and slice the strawberries.

5 Unroll the sponge, spread the fromage frais mixture over the sponge and sprinkle with the sliced strawberries. Roll the sponge up again and transfer to a serving plate. Sprinkle with almonds, lightly dust with icing sugar and serve.

FRUIT & NUT FUDGE

MAKES 36
2 tbsp butter, plus extra for greasing
250 g/9 oz plain chocolate,
　broken into pieces

4 tbsp evaporated milk
450 g/1 lb icing sugar, sifted
50 g/1¾ oz roughly chopped hazelnuts
50 g/1¾ oz sultanas

GRANDMA'S TIPS

Fudge is an old favourite amongst all ages. Add extra nuts or sultanas if you prefer or substitute the hazelnuts for almonds.

1 Lightly grease a 20-cm/8-inch square cake tin.

2 Put the chocolate in a heatproof bowl with the butter and evaporated milk and set over a saucepan of gently simmering water. Stir until the chocolate and butter have melted and the mixture is well blended.

3 Remove the bowl from the heat and gradually beat in the icing sugar. Stir the hazelnuts and sultanas into the mixture. Press the fudge into the prepared tin and smooth the top. Chill until firm.

4 Tip the fudge out onto a chopping board and cut into squares. Chill in the refrigerator until required.

NUTTY FLAPJACKS

MAKES 16

115 g/4 oz butter, plus extra for greasing
200 g/7 oz rolled oats
115 g/4 oz chopped hazelnuts

55 g/2 oz plain flour
2 tbsp golden syrup
85 g/3 oz light muscovado sugar

1 Preheat the oven to 180°C/350°F/Gas Mark 4, then grease a 23-cm/9-inch square ovenproof dish or cake tin. Place the rolled oats, chopped hazelnuts and flour in a large mixing bowl and stir together.

2 Place the butter, syrup and sugar in a saucepan over a low heat and stir until melted. Pour onto the dry ingredients and mix well. Turn the mixture into the prepared ovenproof dish and smooth the surface with the back of a spoon.

3 Bake in the oven for 20–25 minutes, or until golden and firm to the touch. Mark into 16 pieces and leave to cool in the tin. When completely cooled, cut through with a sharp knife and remove from the tin.

LEMON BUTTERFLY CAKES

MAKES 12
115 g/4 oz self-raising flour
½ tsp baking powder
115 g/4 oz butter, softened
115 g/4 oz caster sugar
2 eggs, beaten
finely grated rind of ½ lemon

2–4 tbsp milk
icing sugar, for dusting

filling
55 g/2 oz butter
115 g/4 oz icing sugar
1 tbsp lemon juice

GRANDMA'S TIPS

Cupcakes are always a favourite for children's parties. You can use multi-coloured paper cases to make them look even more attractive. A whole strawberry, raspberry or glacé cherry can be popped on top to decorate.

1 Preheat the oven to 190°C/375°F/Gas Mark 5. Place 12 paper cases in a bun tin. Sift the flour and baking powder into a bowl. Add the butter, sugar, eggs, lemon rind and enough milk to give a medium-soft consistency. Beat the mixture thoroughly until smooth, then divide among the paper cases and bake in the preheated oven for 15–20 minutes, or until well risen and golden. Transfer to wire racks to cool.

2 To make the filling, place the butter in a bowl. Sift in the icing sugar and add the lemon juice. Beat well until smooth and creamy. When the cakes are completely cooled, use a sharp-pointed vegetable knife to cut a circle from the top of each cake, then cut each circle in half.

3 Spoon a little buttercream into the centre of each cake and press the 2 semi-circular pieces into it to resemble wings. Dust the cakes with sifted icing sugar before serving.

BLUEBERRY MUFFINS

MAKES 10–12
250 g/9 oz plain white flour
1 tsp baking powder
pinch of salt
100 g/3½ oz demerara sugar,
    plus 1 tbsp for sprinkling

1 egg, beaten
225 ml/8 fl oz milk
55 g/2 oz unsalted butter, melted
125 g/4½ oz small fresh blueberries

GRANDMA'S TIPS

This classic muffin is ideal for a lazy weekend brunch or a quick and filling breakfast on the way to work.

1 Preheat the oven to 180°C/350°F/Gas Mark 4. Line a 12-hole muffin tin with paper cases. Sift the flour, baking powder and salt into a large bowl and stir in the sugar.

2 Add the beaten egg, milk and melted butter to the dry ingredients and stir in lightly until just combined – do not overmix. Carefully fold in the blueberries.

3 Spoon the mixture into the paper cases, taking care not to overfill, and sprinkle with the remaining sugar.

4 Bake in the preheated oven for 25–30 minutes until golden brown and firm. Transfer to a wire rack to cool a little.

SCONES

MAKES 10–12

450 g/1 lb plain flour,
  plus extra for dusting
½ tsp salt
2 tsp baking powder
55 g/2 oz butter

2 tbsp caster sugar
250 ml/9 fl oz milk
3 tbsp milk, for glazing
strawberry jam and clotted cream,
  to serve

1 Preheat the oven to 220°C/425°F/Gas Mark 7.

2 Sift the flour, salt and baking powder into a bowl. Rub in the butter until the mixture resembles breadcrumbs. Stir in the sugar.

3 Make a well in the centre and pour in the milk. Stir in using a palette knife and make a soft dough.

4 Turn the mixture onto a floured surface and lightly flatten the dough until it is of an even thickness, about 1 cm/½ inch. Don't be heavy-handed, scones need a light touch.

5 Use a 6-cm/2½-inch pastry cutter to cut out the scones and place on the baking tray.

6 Glaze with a little milk and bake for 10–12 minutes, until golden and well risen.

7 Cool on a wire rack and serve freshly baked with strawberry jam and clotted cream.

SHORTBREAD

MAKES 8
115 g/4 oz butter, cut into small pieces,
  plus extra for greasing
175 g/6 oz plain flour,
  plus extra for dusting

pinch of salt
55 g/2 oz caster sugar,
  plus extra for dusting

GRANDMA'S TIPS

*To give shortbread a bit more
texture, replace 55 g/2 oz of
the flour with semolina, which
will give it a more granular,
slightly gritty texture.*

1 Preheat the oven to 150°C/300°F/Gas Mark 2.

2 Grease a 20-cm/8-inch fluted cake tin or flan tin.

3 Mix together the flour, salt and sugar. Rub the butter into the dry ingredients.
Continue to work the mixture until it forms a soft dough. Make sure you do not
overwork the shortbread or it will be tough, not crumbly as it should be.

4 Lightly press the dough into the cake tin. If you don't have a fluted tin, roll out the
dough on a lightly floured board, place on a baking tray and pinch the edges to form a
scalloped pattern.

5 Mark into 8 pieces with a knife. Prick all over with a fork and bake in the centre of the
oven for 45–50 minutes until the shortbread is firm and just coloured.

6 Allow to cool in the tin and dust with the sugar. Cut into portions and remove to a
wire rack. Store in an airtight container in a cool place until needed.

CHOCOLATE CHIP
COOKIES

MAKES 18
125 g/4½ oz soft margarine,
  plus extra for greasing
175 g/6 oz plain flour
1 tsp baking powder

85 g/3 oz light muscovado sugar
5 tbsp caster sugar
½ tsp vanilla essence
1 egg
125 g/4½ oz dark chocolate chips

GRANDMA'S TIPS

*Try different types of chocolate
to add variety. You can use milk
chocolate chips or white chocolate
or even experiment with broken
up chocolate bars. In fact, you
can combine all your favourites
together in one cookie!*

1 Preheat the oven to 190°C/375°F/Gas Mark 5. Lightly grease two baking trays.

2 Place all of the ingredients in a large mixing bowl and beat until well combined.

3 Place tablespoonfuls of the mixture onto the baking trays, spacing them well apart to allow for spreading during cooking.

4 Bake in the preheated oven for 10–12 minutes or until the cookies are golden brown.

5 Using a palette knife, transfer the cookies to a wire rack to cool completely before serving.

ORANGE GINGERNUTS

MAKES 30
125 g/4½ oz butter,
  plus extra for greasing
350 g/12 oz self-raising flour
pinch of salt
200 g/7 oz caster sugar

1 tbsp ground ginger
1 tsp bicarbonate of soda
75 g/2¾ oz golden syrup
1 egg, beaten
1 tsp grated orange rind

1 Preheat the oven to 160°C/325°F/Gas Mark 3. Lightly grease several baking trays.

2 Sieve the flour, salt, sugar, ginger and bicarbonate of soda into a large mixing bowl.

3 Heat the butter and golden syrup together in a saucepan over a very low heat until the butter has melted.

4 Leave the butter mixture to cool slightly, then pour it onto the dry ingredients.

5 Add the egg and orange rind and mix thoroughly.

6 Using your hands, carefully shape the dough into 30 even-sized balls.

7 Place the balls well apart on the prepared baking trays, then flatten them slightly with your fingers.

8 Bake in the preheated oven for 15–20 minutes, then transfer them to a wire rack to cool.

COTTAGE LOAF

MAKES I LARGE LOAF
675 g/1 lb 8 oz strong white bread flour, plus extra for dusting
2 tsp salt

I sachet easy-blend dried yeast
400 ml/14 fl oz lukewarm water
vegetable oil, for brushing

GRANDMA'S TIPS

This bread is great served as part of a ploughman's meal, or served cut into fresh chunks with your favourite soup for a filling lunch.

1 Sift the flour and salt together into a bowl. Add the yeast and stir in. Make a well in the centre, pour in the lukewarm water and stir with a wooden spoon until the dough begins to come together, then knead with your hands until it leaves the side of the bowl. Turn out on to a lightly floured surface and knead for about 10 minutes, until smooth and elastic.

2 Brush a bowl with oil. Shape the dough into a ball, put it in the bowl and put the bowl into a plastic bag or cover with a damp tea towel. Leave to rise in a warm place for 1–2 hours, until the dough has doubled in volume.

3 Brush 2 baking sheets with oil. Turn out the dough on to a lightly floured surface and knock back with your fist. Knead for 2 minutes, then divide the dough into 2 pieces, one about twice the size of the other. Shape each piece into a ball, put them on to the prepared baking sheets and put the baking sheets into plastic bags or cover with damp tea towels. Leave to rise in a warm place for 30 minutes.

4 With a floured hand, gently flatten the larger ball of dough. Cut a 5-cm/2-in cross in the centre of the top and brush with water. Put the smaller ball of dough on top. Make small vertical slashes all around both pieces of dough. Brush the handle of a wooden spoon with the oil and push it into the centre of the loaf so that it makes a hole through both pieces of dough. Put the loaf on the baking sheet into a plastic bag or cover with a damp tea towel. Leave in a warm place for 15 minutes.

5 Meanwhile, preheat the oven to 220°C/425°F/Gas Mark 7. Bake the loaf for 40 minutes, until the crust is golden brown and it sounds hollow when tapped on the base with your knuckles. Transfer to a wire rack to cool.

MIXED SEED BREAD

MAKES I LOAF
375 g/13 oz strong white flour,
  plus extra for dusting
125 g/4½ oz rye flour
I ½ tbsp skimmed milk powder
I ½ tsp salt
I tbsp soft light brown sugar
I tsp easy-blend dried yeast
I ½ tbsp sunflower oil,
  plus extra for greasing

2 tsp lemon juice
300 ml/10 fl oz lukewarm water
I tsp caraway seeds
½ tsp poppy seeds
½ tsp sesame seeds

topping
I egg white
I tbsp water
I tbsp sunflower seeds or pumpkin seeds

GRANDMA'S TIPS

This is an alternative to white or wholemeal bread and is ideal for all your favourite sandwich fillings or delicious for cheese on toast.

1 Place the flours, milk powder, salt, sugar and yeast in a large bowl. Pour in the oil and add the lemon juice and water. Stir in the seeds and mix well to make a smooth dough. Turn out onto a lightly floured surface and knead well for about 10 minutes, until smooth.

2 Brush a bowl with oil. Shape the dough into a ball, place it in the bowl and cover with a damp tea towel. Leave to rise in a warm place for 1 hour, until the dough has doubled in volume.

3 Oil a 900-g/2-lb loaf tin. Turn out the dough onto a lightly floured surface and knead for 1 minute until smooth. Shape the dough the length of the tin and three times the width. Fold the dough in three lengthways and place it in the tin with the join underneath. Cover and leave in a warm place for 30 minutes, until it has risen above the tin.

4 Preheat the oven to 220°C/425°F/Gas Mark 7. For the topping, lightly beat the egg white with the water to make a glaze. Just before baking, brush the glaze over the loaf, then gently press the sunflower seeds all over the top.

5 Bake in the preheated oven for 30 minutes, or until firm and golden brown. Test that the loaf is cooked by tapping on the base with your knuckles – it should sound hollow. Transfer to a wire rack to cool.

WHITE BREAD

MAKES I LARGE LOAF
450 g/1 lb strong white flour, plus 2 tbsp
   for dusting
1 tsp salt

7 g/¼ oz easy-blend dried yeast
1 tbsp vegetable oil or melted butter,
   plus 1 tsp for greasing
300 ml/10 fl oz warm water

1 Mix the flour, salt and yeast together in a mixing bowl. Add the oil and water and stir well to form a soft dough.

2 Turn the dough out onto a lightly floured board and knead well by hand for 5–7 minutes. Alternatively, use a free-standing electric mixer for this and knead the dough with the dough hook for 4–5 minutes. The dough should have a smooth appearance and feel elastic.

3 Return the dough to the bowl, cover with clingfilm and leave to rise in a warm place for 1 hour. When it has doubled in size, turn it out onto a floured board and knead again for 30 seconds; this is known as 'knocking back'. Knead it until smooth.

4 Shape the dough into a rectangle the length of the tin and three times the width. Grease the tin well, fold the dough into three lengthways and put it in the tin with the join underneath for a well-shaped loaf. Cover and leave to rise in a warm place for 30 minutes until it has risen well above the tin.

5 Preheat the oven to 220°C/425°F/Gas Mark 7. Bake in the centre of the preheated oven for 25–30 minutes until firm and golden brown. Test that the loaf is cooked by tapping it on the bottom – it should sound hollow. Cool on a cooling rack for 30 minutes. Store in an airtight container in a cool place for 3–4 days.

Index

almonds
  baked apples 173
  Christmas pudding 134
  strawberry roulade 198
  tiramisu 168
apples
  apple & blackberry crumble 150
  apple pie 144
  apple streusel cake 188
  baked apples 173
apricots: baked apples 173
aubergines
  ratatouille 69
  vegetable cannelloni 63

bacon/pancetta
  bacon butties 18
  beef bourguignon 75
  coq au vin 72
  lasagne al forno 64
  souffléd baked potatoes 50
  spaghetti bolognese 58
  spaghetti carbonara 60
baked apples 173
baked rice pudding 170
bananas
  banana coconut loaf cake 197
  banana splits 176
batter
  fish & chips 38
  toad in the hole 36
beef
  beef bourguignon 75
  beef enchiladas 78
  beef goulash 87
  beef stew with herb
    dumplings 26
  chilli con carne 76
  festive beef Wellington 115
  lasagne al forno 64
  roast beef 24
  shepherd's pie 30
  spaghetti bolognese 58
  spicy beef with black bean
    sauce 94
  steak & kidney pie 29
blackberries: apple & blackberry
  crumble 150
blueberries
  blueberry muffins 206
  blueberry pancakes 174

New York cheesecake with
    blueberry compote 161
brandy snaps 133
bread
  bacon butties 18
  bread & butter pudding 156
  cottage loaf 216
  mixed seed bread 218
  Welsh rarebit 17
  white bread 221
broccoli: salmon fishcakes 42
Brussels sprouts with buttered
    chestnuts 130
butternut squash
  roasted butternut squash
    risotto 47
roasted root vegetables 127

cakes
  apple streusel cake 188
  banana coconut loaf cake 197
  Black Forest gateau 162
  classic carrot cake 186
  coffee & walnut cake 191
  lemon butterfly cakes 204
  lemon drizzle cake 182
  rich fruit cake 185
  strawberry roulade 198
  Victoria sponge cake 180
cannellini beans
  lamb shanks with cannellini
    beans 32
  sausage & bean casserole 35
carrots
  beef bourguignon 75
  classic carrot cake 186
  creamy carrot & parsnip
    soup 100
  lamb shanks with cannellini
    beans 32
  lasagne al forno 64
  roasted root vegetables 127
  shepherd's pie 30
  spaghetti bolognese 58
  winter vegetable cobbler 44
cauliflower
  cauliflower cheese 54
  vegetable korma 82
  winter vegetable cobbler 44
celery
  lamb shanks with cannellini
    beans 32

lasagne al forno 64
  spaghetti bolognese 58
  winter vegetable cobbler 44
cheese
  beef enchiladas 78
  cauliflower cheese 54
  chicken Kiev 84
  lasagne al forno 64
  macaroni cheese 48
  pizza Margherita 66
  souffléd baked potatoes 50
  spaghetti carbonara 60
  vegetable cannelloni 63
  Welsh rarebit 17
  winter vegetable cobbler 44
  see also soft cheese
cherries
  Black Forest gateau 162
  latticed cherry pie 146
chestnuts
  Brussels sprouts with buttered
    chestnuts 130
  chestnut, Madeira & mushroom
    tarts 104
chicken
  chicken Kiev 84
  chicken, mushroom & tarragon
    pie 23
  chicken tikka masala 81
  coq au vin 72
  cream of chicken soup 14
  paella 70
  roast chicken 20
chicken liver pâté 103
chilli con carne 76
chillies
  chicken tikka masala 81
  chilli con carne 76
  vegetable korma 82
chocolate
  banana splits 176
  Black Forest gateau 162
  chocolate chip cookies 212
  fruit & nut fudge 200
  marbled chocolate & orange
    teabread 194
  profiteroles 164
Christmas pudding 134
coconut
  banana coconut loaf cake 197
  carrot cake 186
  chicken tikka masala 81

coffee
  coffee & walnut cake 191
  tiramisù 168
coq au vin 72
cottage loaf 216
courgettes: ratatouille 69
cranberries
  mixed nut roast with cranberry
    & red wine sauce 121
  rich fruit cake 185
cream of chicken soup 14
creamy carrot & parsnip soup 100
custard
  festive sherry trifle 136
  spotted dick & custard 167

dates
  rich fruit cake 185
  sticky toffee pudding 158
dried fruit
  bread & butter pudding 156
  Christmas pudding 134
  coffee & walnut cake 191
  fruit & nut fudge 200
  rich fruit cake 185
  spotted dick & custard 167
  sticky toffee pudding 158

eggs: spaghetti carbonara 60

festive beef Wellington 115
festive mince pies 139
festive sherry trifle 136
fish & seafood
  fish & chips 38
  fisherman's pie 41
  see also prawns; salmon
fisherman's pie 41
French beans: pork chow mein 93
fruit & nut fudge 200

gingerbread 192
glazed gammon 112
glazed turnips 124
golden syrup
  brandy snaps 133
  gingerbread 192
  nutty flapjacks 203
  orange gingernuts 215
goose: Yuletide goose with
    honey & pears 110

gravy 24

ham
  glazed gammon 112
  souffléd baked potatoes 50
hazelnuts
  fruit & nut fudge 200
  mixed nut roast with cranberry
    & red wine sauce 121
  nutty flapjacks 203
herb dumplings 26
honey
  baked apples 173
  honeyed parsnips 128
  roasted butternut squash
    risotto 47
  Yuletide goose with honey &
    pears 110

ice cream
  banana splits 176
  rich vanilla ice cream 155

jus 24

kidney beans: chilli con carne 76

lamb
  lamb shanks with cannellini
    beans 32
  rack of lamb 116
  shepherd's pie 30
lasagne al forno 64
latticed cherry pie 146
leeks
  beef bourguignon 75
  cream of chicken soup 14
  leek & potato soup 12
  wild mushroom & sherry
    soup 98
lemons
  lemon butterfly cakes 204
  lemon drizzle cake 182
  lemon meringue pie 152
lentils: winter vegetable
    cobbler 44

macaroni cheese 48
marbled chocolate & orange
    teabread 194
mixed seed bread 218

mushrooms
  beef bourguignon 75
  beef goulash 87
  chestnut, Madeira & mushroom
    tarts 104
  chicken, mushroom & tarragon
    pie 23
  coq au vin 72
  festive beef Wellington 115
  fisherman's pie 41
  mushroom stroganoff 88
  spicy beef with black bean
    sauce 94
  vegetable cannelloni 63
  wild mushroom & sherry
    soup 98
  winter vegetable cobbler 44

New York cheesecake with
    blueberry compote 161
nuts
  banana splits 176
  mixed nut roast with cranberry
    & red wine sauce 121
  pear & pecan strudel 149
  see also almonds; chestnuts;
    hazelnuts; walnuts
nutty flapjacks 203

oats
  baked apples 173
  nutty flapjacks 203
oranges
  lamb shanks with cannellini
    beans 32
  marbled chocolate & orange
    teabread 194
  orange gingernuts 215
  pear & pecan strudel 149
  spiced Christmas punch 140

paella 70
parsnips
  creamy carrot & parsnip
    soup 100
  honeyed parsnips 128
  roasted root vegetables 127
pasta
  lasagne al forno 64
  macaroni cheese 48
  spaghetti bolognese 58

spaghetti carbonara 60
vegetable cannelloni 63
pastry
  apple pie 144
  chestnut, Madeira & mushroom
    tarts 104
  chicken, mushroom & tarragon
    pie 23
  festive beef Wellington 115
  festive mince pies 139
  latticed cherry pie 146
  lemon meringue pie 152
  pear & pecan strudel 149
  profiteroles 164
  smoked salmon, dill &
    horseradish tartlets 106
  steak & kidney pie 29
pears
  pear & pecan strudel 149
  Yuletide goose with honey &
    pears 110
peas: chicken, mushroom &
  tarragon pie 23
peppers
  beef goulash 87
  chilli con carne 76
  paella 70
  ratatouille 69
  sausage & bean casserole 35
  vegetable korma 82
pizza Margherita 66
poached salmon 118
pork
  paella 70
  pork chow mein 93
potatoes
  fish & chips 38
  fisherman's pie 41
  leek & potato soup 12
  perfect mash 53
  perfect roast potatoes 122
  salmon fishcakes 42
  shepherd's pie 30
  souffléd baked potatoes 50
  vegetable korma 82
prawns
  fisherman's pie 41
  paella 70
  sweet & sour prawns 90
profiteroles 164
ratatouille 69

rice
  baked rice pudding 170
  paella 70
  roasted butternut squash
    risotto 47
roast beef 24
roast chicken 20
roast turkey with stuffing 109
roasted butternut squash
  risotto 47
roasted root vegetables 127

salmon
  poached salmon 118
  salmon fishcakes 42
  smoked salmon, dill &
    horseradish tartlets 106
sausages
  paella 70
  sausage & bean casserole 35
  toad in the hole 36
scones 209
shepherd's pie 30
shortbread 210
smoked salmon, dill &
  horseradish tartlets 106
soft cheese
  classic carrot cake 186
  New York cheesecake with
    blueberry compote 161
  tiramisù 168
souffléd baked potatoes 50
soups
  cream of chicken soup 14
  creamy carrot & parsnip
    soup 100
  leek & potato soup 12
  wild mushroom & sherry
    soup 98
spaghetti bolognese 58
spaghetti carbonara 60
spiced Christmas punch 140
spicy beef with black bean
  sauce 94
spinach: vegetable cannelloni 63
spotted dick & custard 167
steak & kidney pie 29
sticky toffee pudding 158
strawberries
  festive sherry trifle 136
  strawberry roulade 198

swede: winter vegetable
  cobbler 44
sweet & sour prawns 90
sweet potatoes
  roasted root vegetables 127
  wild mushroom & sherry
    soup 98
sweetcorn: spicy beef with black
  bean sauce 94

tiramisù 168
toad in the hole 36
tomatoes
  beef goulash 87
  chicken tikka masala 81
  chilli con carne 76
  lamb shanks with cannellini
    beans 32
  lasagne al forno 64
  paella 70
  pizza Margherita 66
  ratatouille 69
  sausage & bean casserole 35
  spaghetti bolognese 58
  vegetable cannelloni 63
  vegetable korma 82
  winter vegetable cobbler 44
tortillas: beef enchiladas 78
turkey
  roast turkey with stuffing 109
  souffléd baked potatoes 50
turnips
  glazed turnips 124
  roasted root vegetables 127

vegetable cannelloni 63
vegetable korma 82
Victoria sponge cake 180

walnuts
  classic carrot cake 186
  coffee & walnut cake 191
  mixed nut roast with cranberry
    & red wine sauce 121
Welsh rarebit 17
White bread 221
wild mushroom & sherry soup 98
winter vegetable cobbler 44

Yuletide goose with honey &
  pears 110